D1715294

The Fig Tree Revolution

The Fig Tree Revolution

Unleashing Local Churches into the Mission of Justice

Bill Mefford

CASCADE *Books* • Eugene, Oregon

THE FIG TREE REVOLUTION
Unleashing Local Churches into the Mission of Justice

Cascade Books
An Imprint of Wipf and Stock Publishers
199 W. 8th Ave., Suite 3
Eugene, OR 97401

www.wipfandstock.com

PAPERBACK ISBN: 978-1-5326-1670-9
HARDCOVER ISBN: 978-1-4982-4064-2
EBOOK ISBN: 978-1-4982-4063-5

Cataloguing-in-Publication data:

Names: Mefford, Bill.

Title: The fig tree revolution : unleashing local churches into the mission of justice / Bill Mefford.

Description: Eugene, OR : Cascade Books, 2017 | Includes bibliographical references.

Identifiers: ISBN 978-1-5326-1670-9 (paperback) | ISBN 978-1-4982-4064-2 (hardcover) | ISBN 978-1-4982-4063-5 (ebook)

Subjects: LCSH: Mission of the church. | Kingdom of God.

Classification: BV601.8 .M44 2017 (print) | BV601.8 .M44 (ebook)

Manufactured in the U.S.A.   10/12/17

To the Rapid Response Team and all the United Methodists from local churches I have worked with for over the last decade, this book is for you.

Thanks for letting me walk with you on this journey toward justice.

Contents

Preface

For more than a decade I had the immeasurable joy of working alongside people of faith, primarily United Methodists, in local churches as we struggled for justice on a plethora of issues. I have worked with people in local churches who are either directly impacted by injustice themselves or who are serving and attending churches that are immersed in relationships with people directly impacted. Building upon the foundation of my dissertation, my interaction with them has greatly shaped and formed much of what I have shared in the trainings I've led throughout the country. I have learned so much from people experiencing injustice firsthand it is impossible to measure. I am forever grateful for the lessons that I have learned and this book is the manifestation of those trainings I have led and continue to lead.

In the last few years, several people have asked me to write down the material I've used for the trainings, but I always hesitated to do so. My main hesitation was my lack of time and my preference for doing the work rather than writing about it. However, with an unanticipated break in my life and schedule in January of 2016, I started writing. I did not start out to write a book; it was simply therapeutic to write. But the writing turned into this effort, and this is the product.

My hope for this project is simple. I want this to be something of a guidebook for groups, teams, or networks located in local churches that want to engage in advocacy and organizing. For far too long, especially in mainline denominations, advocacy and organizing efforts have been institutionally relegated to a small contingent of people who are deeply committed, but who also seem to exist on the margins of the church. Advocating and organizing for justice is thus not seen as normative among most church people since it has been institutionally marginalized and thus, little is accomplished. We must make advocacy and organizing for justice normative in the worship, witness, and mission of the church if the gospel is to have transformative power in the lives of people who are daily crushed by poverty and oppression.

It is also important to describe what this book will not provide. This is not an exegetical work on the book of Esther. I am looking at the first four chapters of Esther. This book contains reflections on the many lessons that I believe the book of Esther offers us as we consider the work of justice so I am reading it toward that purpose alone. I will look at the primary characters of the book: at their actions, their emotions, and even when possible, their thoughts and motivations.[1] We know the characters of Esther mainly because of what we see them do and say. I hope by observing their actions and statements we can find meaning for our own missional work, particularly for how we respond to injustice in our communities and in our world. I believe Esther has many lessons that can shape how we respond to injustice in ways that will make our engagement in advocacy and organizing more meaningful and transformative.

Faithfulness to the gospel means we must place advocacy and organizing for justice in the center of the praxis of our faith and especially in the discipling and equipping of current and future leaders of the church. Currently, it is not. The struggles for justice we engage in demand that we push ourselves to actually change the systems that perpetuate injustice and oppression. We must no longer be content with only "raising awareness" about injustice.

1. Looking at the characters of the book of Esther has good precedent from one of the book's preeminent scholars, Michael V. Fox. He has written, "All we know about anyone besides ourselves is pieced together from things they do and say . . . and from things other say about them. We sort through these bits and pieces, looking for (and creating) order and meaning." *Character and Ideology*, 7.

We must stop injustice. To do this we need greater access to these crucial forms of missional engagement by the whole body of Christ, and not just relegate this engagement to small committees or certain organizations. I pray folks who have little prior engagement, or no prior activity at all in this type of mission will find the work of justice accessible through this book. I pray you and the people in your congregation might even be motivated from hearing the amazing (and true!) stories in these chapters. And I pray new leaders will discover new and creative dreams that can be fulfilled through learning from the lessons of Esther and Mordecai. It is truly a time for new dreams, new connections, and new leaders.

Jesus has called us to change the world and we need to start now. That means today.

One term I want to unpack briefly before we get any farther is the word, "missiological." This will be found in various forms throughout the book. Essentially, missiology refers to the study of the mission of the Church. There is much in the history of the mission of the Church that has sadly been detrimental to people, especially indigenous people, who were often the objects of the church's mission. Colonialism, fusion of the church's interests with the interests of militaristic governments, and injustice against vulnerable groups marks much of the church's missiological history. At the same time, the missional engagement of the church has also brought out the most faithful witness of the gospel, especially as followers of Jesus have chosen solidarity with those who are directly impacted by societal injustice. Therefore, when I use the terms, "missiological" or "missional" it will be with the latter thoughts in mind; urging us as followers of Jesus to more closely reflect God's faithful love for all of creation by choosing solidarity with those experiencing injustice. Being missional is at heart being relational in the most healthy, productive, and mutually transformative way.

This book is divided into two parts. The first part is located in chapters 1 through 4, and the emphasis here will be on reflections gleaned from various sections of Esther 1–4. Before we move into the actions steps I want us to reflect theologically on what participating in justice really means, using the story and the characters of Esther as examples to better see and understand our current context. Our reflection will make our action more informed and effective.

Chapters 5 through 8 make up the second part of the book and will focus on our active missional engagement in justice. I am using the word "steps" in naming chapters 4-8 because I see the content in those chapters as important steps for our journey into advocating and organizing for justice. I do not in any way want this to be thought of as a formula though. Formulas can be dangerous because it takes one contextual approach and makes it normative for all contexts no matter the differences. Instead, I think it wise to learn from one another through the sharing of stories of how justice has been achieved (or not achieved), while constantly seeking to contextualize the lessons we learn from those stories to our local communities. I hope the lessons from Esther and the stories I share will fuel your creativity and your dreams. The work of justice is far too important to mindlessly follow the examples of others. It is up to you and those I hope you will be reading this with to do the important work of contextualization.

This book can be read individually, but is meant to be read by teams of people who share a vision and passion for concrete change for and with people experiencing injustice or oppression. To help toward that end, I have included discussion questions along with possible ideas for missiological engagement at the end of each chapter. Please take note that I am offering ideas—again, not formulaic steps. It is crucial that you and your team contextualize these ideas into meaningful and helpful practices that move you along in your journeys toward the work of advocacy and organizing. Some of these steps might require a reasonable amount of time to plan, while others will simply be creative ways to provide deeper reflection and open dialogue.

Lastly, I also would love to know how your church or small group uses this book to help make change alongside those directly impacted by injustice. Hearing stories of what folks are doing to change the world is my favorite part of this whole effort! I am part of a network of progressive dreamers, innovators, and organizers called Fig Tree Revolution. We would love to have you join us and share with us what you are doing to engage in the struggle to achieve justice in our world. You can reach me at Bill@FigTreeRevolution.com and we are on Facebook as well. (www.figtreerevolution.com)

I want to walk with you as we confront together the terrible injustices that blot our world and also as we experience the inexplicable joy and hope Jesus showers on us as we work with him to love and transform the world.

So, what do you say? Do you want to change the world together?

Acknowledgments

Though this book bears my name, and so I am credited for any and all of its faults, the real credit for any good this book might promote belongs to many people. Through all of the trainings I have led and the constant travel, my amazing family was always supportive and encouraging. My wife, Marti, and two sons, Eli and Isaiah embody God's grace and love for me more than they will ever know. Thank you.

I'm also extremely grateful for the support I received from the staff at Cascade Books. I am especially grateful for the work of Charlie Collier, Brian Palmer, and Calvin Jaffarian, and the excellent work of Sallie Vandagrift. Thank you for making this process so enjoyable.

I learned so many things from so many people but I especially want to thank Kristin Kumpf, the best organizer I have ever seen or known. Keep building, your work is not in vain.

The ideas for this book began with my years of serving in local churches in Texas and Kentucky and in the dissertation I wrote under the mentorship of Dr. Mike Rynkiewich. Mike was a mentor in every sense of the word and I continue to value his wisdom and friendship.

This book is dedicated to the grassroots United Methodists with whom I worked so closely and learned so much, but I want to mention several people in particular. One of the readers whose comments were instrumental was Greg Leffel, a good friend and a brilliant mind from whom I have learned so much about the mission of the church. I also am thankful for the interview time given me by Beth Reilly and Emily Sutton, both of whom are amazing in their service for God and love of people. The reading group read through the book, made suggested changes, and then joined me on a conference call to talk through the suggested changes. Even more, they kept encouraging me long after their commitment was done. These are amazing leaders in the church and even better friends. They include: Andrea Paret (whose help was over and above what I could have hoped for), Anika Jones, Alejandro Alfaro-Santiz, Paul Fleck, Elizabeth Murray, and Brenda Vaca. Thank you guys for everything.

The Story

To set the stage and give us a common narrative to work from, I am retelling the story from the first four chapters in Esther. The lessons we will glean in this book do not necessarily follow sequentially from the biblical text so this allows us to have a common knowledge of the story before we begin to draw wisdom from it. I am basing my interpretation of it from the New Revised Standard Version.

Chapter 1

When Israel was ruled by the powerful Persian King Ahasuerus, the king threw an enormous banquet for all of the officials in the palace, as well as for all the citizens of Susa, the capital city. It was an opportunity for the king to show off his wealth so there was an enormous amount of food and drink made available. The party lasted seven days. On the last day, when the king and all of his buddies were good and filled with food and drink from a full week of partying, he called for Queen Vashti to come and be viewed by everyone he had gathered because she was beautiful and he wanted to show her off.

Queen Vashti, who had thrown her own party for the women in the palace, refused to come. The king was deeply offended and angry and so he checked with his palace officials to see how he needed to respond. He was not used to being disobeyed by anyone. The officials advised the king that she not only disrespected the king by refusing to obey his command, she disrespected all of the officials in the palace, who, not coincidentally were all male. They feared a massive uprising by the women in the kingdom, specifically their own wives. Therefore, they urged an edict to be issued to punish Queen Vashti for not coming into the king's presence by never being allowed into the king's presence again. Her position was to be given to another and all women throughout the kingdom were ordered to give honor to their husbands.

That sounded about right to the king so he did it.

Chapter 2

As a result of the dismissal of Vashti, a massive search was made for her replacement. A young woman named Esther, adopted and raised by her uncle Mordecai, was found and won the heart of the king who gave her her own maids and servants and brought her into the palace. Under the guidance of Mordecai, Esther did not tell the king she was Jewish. Esther was greatly loved by the king and she eventually took the position of Queen Vashti.

One day when Mordecai was standing outside the palace gate, which is where he came regularly to hear the important business of the day and to check in on Esther, he overheard two palace officials conspiring to assassinate the king. Mordecai shared what he heard with Esther who in turn told the king and the conspiracy was foiled. Both men were hanged and the king was saved.

Chapter 3

After this event the king promoted Haman, an official in the king's court, to the number two position in the kingdom. Haman was taught hatred for the Jews from his childhood by his father. So, after his promotion was made public, everyone outside the palace gate bowed down in homage to Haman except Mordecai. Haman was so infuriated by Mordecai's insolence he was tempted to assault him, but because Mordecai was so beneath him in his social and political status he devised another way to get revenge, especially when he found out that Mordecai was Jewish, a group of people he had long hated.

A short time later Haman put his plot into action. Haman started out by describing to the king a people who were spread throughout all of the provinces of the kingdom. He did not name who these people were; he kept their identity unknown at first. This people, claimed Haman, refused to obey the laws of the kingdom for they had their own laws. Haman suggested they should not be tolerated and that the king should allow an edict to be issued calling for their destruction. In return, Haman would pay a large amount of money directly into the king's treasury. The king assented to Haman's plans and letters were sent to all the provinces in the kingdom calling for the annihilation of all the Jews and the looting of their possessions.

As the edict of the coming genocide of the Jewish people was read Haman and the king sat down to enjoy a drink together and the entire city of Susa was thrown into confusion.

Chapter 4

Upon hearing the edict Mordecai tore his clothes, put on sackcloth and ashes, and publicly mourned at the city gate. This was done in every province where the edict was read. Esther could not see her uncle publicly grieving as she was hidden in the palace, but her maids and servants reported to her what he was doing. Upon hearing his condition, she sent down clothes for him to change into. He refused to take the clothes.

So, Esther sent down Hathach, her servant, to find out why Mordecai was publicly mourning. Mordecai explained to Hathach all that Haman had done and gave him a copy of the edict that had been read in Susa. He urged Esther to approach the king and advocate for the safety of her people. When Hathach told Esther all that Mordecai had shared with him, she sent a message back to Mordecai reminding him that anyone who approaches the king without being summoned is to be put to death unless the king extends his scepter to them.

Again through Hathach, Mordecai reminded Esther that though she lived in the palace she would not survive the violence being directed against the Jews. She remained Jewish no matter her status. "Perhaps," he told her, "you have come into the position you are in for such a time as this."

Convinced by what her uncle had told her, she commanded that he organize all the Jews in Susa, have them fast for her for three days and she will do the same with her servants in the palace. Then, she will approach the king and advocate for her people. If she perishes, then she perishes, was her mindset. And Mordecai did as she ordered him.

Reflection

1

The Real Problem of Poverty and Oppression

The first time I saw the power of the story of Esther to mobilize local churches into effective organizing and advocacy was several years ago when I was asked to lead a training for Latino/a United Methodists working on immigration reform. I knew I had more to learn from them than they from me so I shared the first part of the story of Esther and then facilitated a discussion around the many lessons that this story has to teach us. It was a powerful conversation as we spent much of our time talking about the ideas and lessons you will be reading about in this book. During a break one of the men came to me, grabbed my hands in his, looked deeply into my eyes, and passionately proclaimed, "I am Mordecai. You are Mordecai. We are Mordecai." In that brief exchange lay the seeds of creating a typology based on the first four chapters of Esther; a story that reminds us that people directly impacted by injustice are truly called to be the ones who lead us in overcoming injustice as we live into God's dreams of peace, liberation, and genuine security for all people.

Surprisingly, though Esther resounds theologically with so many themes found throughout Scripture, this is the only book in the Bible that never actually mentions the name of God. However, evidence of God's presence is replete throughout the first four chapters in the expressions of worship, the actions of the story's main characters, and in the ultimate rescue of God's people from destruction. Though Mordecai never states God's name, he is confident in his pleading for Esther's action that deliverance would rise from another place if she herself failed to act (4:14).

Though there was some discussion as to whether this book deserved to be included in the Old Testament canon[1] I think we should be glad it is. God's compassion for those who are most vulnerable and God's faithful presence to God's people are evident throughout. I believe the story of Esther shows that with or without verbal proclamation God receives glory when justice is attained, oppression is thwarted, the vulnerable are protected, and grassroots movements are built from the ground up.

Introducing the Players

The story of the first four chapters of Esther is laid out. Now, we need to look at the primary players in the story. Whatever lessons we learn from the author of this book (whose identity we do not know) are conveyed through the struggles, hopes, dreams, fears, and especially actions of the characters in this story. Wisdom emerges from the convergence of seeing how these complex characters act and react within their historical and cultural contexts while we contextualize their actions for our own context.

Esther

We start with who the book is named after. Esther is the primary protagonist in the story for the Jewish people—her people. She is the niece of Mordecai with whom she works closely to bring about justice. She was raised by Mordecai so they share a very personal history that will come into play as this story develops. She is beautiful and intelligent and above all, brave as she risks her

1. The book was not found in the earliest list of canonical books for the Old Testament, but by the dawn of the Christian era it was secure in its placement. It has been widely debated as to the theological value of the book, which is beyond the scope of this study, but there are many who believe there is much we can draw from its pages theologically and of course missiologically. Gaebelein, *Expositors Commentary*, 4:782–84.

life to save her people who are spread throughout the provinces of the Persian Kingdom.

Esther's character has stirred debate historically. Was she the brave and selfless heroine who should be revered in history or was she a mostly compliant subject of a patriarchal and oppressively sexist social order? In several places Esther seems more impacted by those around her—especially when those actors are male—than she is depicted influencing others:

- She was "taken in" by Mordecai when her father and mother died (2:7).

- She again was "taken in" by the king's palace and put under charge of one of the king's eunuchs when he brought in a number of young women into his harem (2:8).

- She dutifully "obeyed" Mordecai all her life, including when he instructed her to keep her ethnicity private (2:10).

On the other hand, this story shows Esther to be someone who rose above her designed place within a patriarchy. She directed her eunuch, Hathach, to deliver messages to Mordecai in regard to the impending holocaust for which he was publicly grieving outside the city gate (4:9). She also "instructed" her uncle to organize the Jews to fast and pray for her as she approached the king to advocate for her people. In fact, the text says, "Mordecai went away and did everything as Esther had *ordered* him" (4:16–17, italics mine).

While it is easy to judge historical characters based on twenty-first century values I find much to admire about Esther, especially considering her actions in the context of what we will see was a paternalist, sexist, and repressive social and political order. I urge those of us reading this story to learn from the actions of all the characters in this story who are not only acting to shape their context, but who are also shaped by their context at the same time.

Esther's rise in the King's palace comes after the king deposes her predecessor, Queen Vashti. She is ousted because she refuses to come when the king orders her to appear before him and his buddies after they had spent a week partying. Vashti repudiates his objectification of her for his vanity and as a result, creates quite an uproar for the king and his court.

The king's advisors feared that Vashti's act of disobedience would inspire other women in the kingdom, especially their own wives. So, they decided to make her punishment an example in order to reinforce the already existing patriarchy. Vashti was banned from ever coming before the King again, thereby setting the stage for the national search in which Esther would be found. It is important to note that the search was for "the girl who pleases the king . . . instead of Vashti." (2:4) The characterization of the search carried the unmistakable meaning that "pleasing the king" meant unquestionable submission to the king. Thus, when Esther ultimately approaches the king she is openly challenging the socially and politically designated place for women to occupy. She is challenging an entrenched patriarchy. She refuses to be defined in such a limited way. This is who Esther is.

King Ahasuerus

Now we turn to the player with the most power; the king. King Ahasuerus is certainly a powerful and wealthy king, though somewhat insecure and quite frankly, not very intelligent. Michael Fox succinctly states it when describing the king and his advisors: "Buffoons rule the empire."[2] The Hebrew name of Ahasuerus has been positively identified as King Xerxes, though, for our purposes we will use the name used in the book, Ahasuerus.

We see the king's "buffoonery" early on as he "punishes" Queen Vashti for refusing to come into his presence by granting her what she seems to have wanted all along—she is forever banned from his presence! The king is so vain he believes the greatest punishment anyone could receive would be to be banned from his presence. Regardless, Ahasuerus was King of Persia and at the beginning of Esther the extent of his dominion is defined: "the same Ahasuerus who ruled over one hundred twenty seven

2. Fox, *Character and Ideology*, 25.

provinces from India to Ethiopia" (1:1). Though his power was extensive, it was also quite fragile as seen in the frantic response to Queen Vashti over her simple refusal to come when he called.

Haman

Our third player was the number two man in the kingdom and also the antagonist. Haman is a bad guy who earns the title. He is a bureaucrat in the king's palace who achieves a level of power second only to that of the king. To celebrate this exultant promotion, Haman decides to organize his own love fest. Whether it was planned or spontaneous, all the King's servants at the city gate bowed down in homage to Haman for his promotion, except for one person.

Mordecai

And yes, that brings us to our last major player in this story. Mordecai refused to bow down to Haman, though the text never says exactly why. It is possible that Mordecai is following the commandment of placing no other gods before Yahweh (Exod 20:3). This follows a theme that can be traced throughout this story; the love shared between God and God's people, even though God's name is never specifically mentioned. For whatever reason Mordecai refuses to bow; he disrespects Haman and it drives Haman over the edge.

Looking at his actions here in a vacuum we might assume that Mordecai is somewhat rebellious. Without a deeper look Mordecai's actions could be understood as resentment of the Persians' rule of his people. However, when we look at the larger context of the first four chapters we see that earlier it was Mordecai who hears news of a plan to assassinate King Ahasuerus while he is at the city gate (2:21-23). In a scene foreshadowing the advocacy that will come later to save the Jews, Mordecai passes this important information on to Esther who shares this with the king and the plot is ultimately foiled. If Mordecai was rebellious or resentful at the general powerlessness of his people, then all Mordecai had to do once he heard the news of the assassination plot was nothing. Without a finger lifted the assassination would have likely been attempted and possibly successful. But Mordecai seeks to do right for all people, even those whom he lives in subjugation to.

Lesson: The Problem with Poverty and Oppression

And here we come to an important lesson that we must recognize before we go any further into this story. The writer of the book does not frame this book around the story of a rebellious Jewish man who refused to respect his God-ordained authorities and unnecessarily places his people in peril. Not at all. The problem in this story is not placed upon the shoulders of the Jewish people. The problem is not with the poor and oppressed, in other words. The writer of this book sees the problem in this story as an abuse of power. The problem is solely placed on Haman and the power structure from which he benefits.

Thus, the framing of this story is akin to the framing of poverty and oppression that runs throughout the majority of Scripture. The problem of poverty is not with the poor and the problem of oppression is not with the oppressed. Though there are exceptions here and there, especially in some of the wisdom literature which was written when Israel was at its zenith of security and power (books like Psalms and Proverbs stand out here), the problem of poverty in most of Scripture is due to an unjust distribution of resources. And the problem of oppression in most of Scripture has to do with the abuse of power by those in powerful positions.

One reason why this is especially important for us today is that this framework for approaching poverty and oppression has been turned upside down, especially by those in the North American church. Far too many members of local churches in North America are unaware of the biblical framing of the root causes of poverty and oppression and instead believe that the problems of poverty and oppression are caused by the poor or oppressed themselves. Thus, the social, political, and economic systems remain intact and ministries that flow from churches that operate within this framework focus on the reformation of the individual and not the society. Individuals are easier to reform and easier to scapegoat, as we will see in this story, than are the larger societal structures that create impoverished and oppressed communities.

Ask yourselves, in many if not most of our current political discussions, who is most often blamed for the problems besetting society? It is the poor. It is vulnerable groups that often exist on the fringes of society. The poor and oppressed are often the least benefitted by economic policies that are most often aimed at "the middle class" by politicians seeking election. Then, during times when the economy turns sour, the poor and oppressed are the first ones to feel the negative effects and they are often blamed for society's failings. Ignoring the poor and oppressed unless they can be used to scapegoat for social problems is effective politics because the poor have no effective lobby or organized political voice.

For instance, some of the most common messages we have heard in recent years from political leaders and in the media (and sometimes even in the church!) are along these lines:

- It is the fault of the immigrants who bring down wages and "steal our jobs."

- It is the poor and homeless who are too lazy to get jobs in the first place thus becoming a financial drain on the government.

- It is the fault of the victim of sexual assault who wore too skimpy an outfit or was too flirtatious with his/her attacker.

- It is the fault of the young black male who was shot by the police for "mouthing off" or for walking in the middle of the street instead of the sidewalk.

Whatever the situation, it seems that the fault of poverty or oppression is consistently assigned to the poor or oppressed—to the most vulnerable and the most ignored, rather than those who benefit from their impoverishment and oppression.

While corporations win multi-million dollar contracts from the government for services, Congress always seems ready to place heavy regulations on the poorest recipients of necessary social services because the poor and oppressed rarely have an effective lobby speaking on their behalf when budgets are being appropriated behind closed doors. Any attempt to initiate regulations on corporations that will protect the climate or prevent too great an accumulation of resources by too few are often seen as attacks on the stability of society or an attempt to divide people against one another. The rare politician who does speak for the need to protect the poor and most vulnerable has often been blamed with instigating "class warfare."

Let's look at an example. In 2003 President Bush signed into law the Medicare Modernization Act. One of the primary provisions of this legislation was to subsidize the costs of prescription drugs. One of the criticisms that has arisen since this bill was enacted is that the bill does not allow for the federal government to negotiate the costs of the drugs with the drug companies for they decide the price. Score one for the pharmaceutical lobby. In fact, Steve Kroft, a journalist with the television show, *60 Minutes,* reported in 2007 that the legislation was largely written by the pharmaceutical lobbyists themselves and was passed at 3 am so as to keep it out of sight from the public. At the time of its passage more than 1,000 pharmaceutical lobbyists were registered to work on this issue. That is 2 lobbyists for every single member of Congress. The cost of all of the lobbying was big: over $10 million. The payoff was even bigger though. The bill cost over $500 billion over the first ten years and much of that went into the pockets of the pharmaceutical companies.[3]

To show how the political game is played for the benefit for those in power, shortly after piloting the bill through the House, Representative Bill Tauzin, a Republican from Louisiana, was made CEO of the pharmaceutical lobby, Pharmaceutical Research and Manufacturers of America, otherwise known

3. Transcript of this segment can be found at: http://www.cbsnews.com/news/under-the-influence/.

as PhRMA (pronounced Pharma). He left Congress to head PhRMA in 2004, the year after the Medicare Modernization Act was signed into law. As CEO of PhRMA Tauzin made millions of dollars, a reward for his work to get the bill passed. However, Tauzin's millions were just a drop in the bucket compared to the billions of dollars pharmaceutical companies have received as a result of the legislation's passage.[4]

The revolving door for members of Congress moving from public service to lobbying firms to cash in for their allegiance to powerful corporate interests is not matched anywhere among those looking out for the concerns of the poor. Perhaps this is why when it comes to debates in the halls of Congress regarding access to crucial social services for the poor there is either political demonization of the poor or simply ignorance of the plight the poor and oppressed face altogether. Because of the lack of political payoff, there are precious few members of Congress who are willing to defend the poor and speak against the millions of dollars being spent to protect the interests of the affluent.

Lesson: The Historical Damage of Classifying the Poor as "Deserving" or "Undeserving"

When we fail to follow the examples of Scripture and blame the poor and oppressed for the problems of poverty and oppression, we will seek to justify our culturally ascribed interpretations by inventing categorizations of the poor. Michael Katz identifies these categories as "deserving" poor and "undeserving" poor.[5]

4. More information on Tauzin can be found here, http://www.bloomberg. com/news/articles/2011-11-29/tauzin-s-11-6-million-made-him-highest-paid-health-law-lobbyist, and his ultimate downfall as CEO of PhRMA for his role in the passage of Obamacare, http://www.nytimes.com/2010/02/13/ health/policy/13pharm.html.

5. Katz locates one of the first attempts historically to separate the "deserving" poor from the "undeserving" poor to the mid-nineteenth century. It was not coincidence that this was at the same time as the rise of the Industrial Revolution when there was an increasing chasm between the rich and the poor in the United States. The first source Katz found in the United States dates

Though the majority of passages in Scripture make no distinction between "deserving" and "undeserving" poor, current approaches in many local churches today are often based on viewing the problem of poverty or oppression as the problems assigned to the poor and oppressed themselves. Very little attention is given to discussing the causes of poverty and oppression, and even less attention is given to actively addressing the systemic causes of poverty and oppression. We help those we deem to be "deserving" and we judge those deemed to be "undeserving" to be outside our ability or interest to aid. Further, we often fail to address the systems of injustice that create poverty or oppression in the first place.

An unjust status quo will remain unchallenged when those in powerful positions who benefit from the status quo reside in the comfortably, detached communities of affluence while tithing to the top-heavy, bureaucratic denominations which plant churches in those detached and comfortable communities. No one wins if we challenge social injustice in this scenario. So, we pacify our consciences by "helping" the poor we regard as "deserving," feeling saintly because we did not do what we usually do which is to ignore the poor altogether.

Let me offer an example. In the early 1990s when I was a youth pastor, fresh out of college, serving in a United Methodist church in a small West Texas town, I remember one day a young Latino couple with a small baby who came to the door of the church asking for help. It was obvious that the man had been beaten up. Though they spoke little English and I never asked (or cared for that matter), they were likely undocumented immigrants for they were clearly afraid to go to any authorities to report the violence they had suffered. For whatever reason, his boss had

---

back to 1821 in Massachusetts when Josiah Quincy, Speaker of Massachusetts' House of Representatives, gave a report on the "poor laws." In his report he suggested that the poor be divided into "two classes . . . the impotent poor; in which denomination are included all, who are wholly incapable of work, through old age, infancy, sickness or corporeal ability . . . [and in the second category] the able poor . . . all who are capable of work, of some nature, or other; but differing in the degree of their capacity, and in the kind of work in which they are capable." Katz, *Undeserving Poor*, 12.

beaten him up and kicked both of them out of where they were living. They were homeless and jobless. They were poor and oppressed. The image of a young couple far from their home, victims of violence and on the run with a small baby was not lost on me as I remembered the story of the flight of Joseph, Mary, and Jesus into Egypt when Jesus was still a baby. Even though I had just started in full-time ministry, the passage, "Whosoever does unto the least of these does unto me" rang in my ears.

I got to work alerting the members of my church to the plight of this young couple. I remember being very intentional in describing their story as sympathetically as possible, even explicitly drawing comparisons to Joseph, Mary, and Jesus when I was asked why we should help them. Though no one in the church knew the young family personally they responded faithfully and energetically. In one day I was able to find them low-cost housing for several months, two weeks of groceries, free health care for his wounds, and a low-wage job where he would at least be treated with a measure of integrity.

Happy ending, right? For them yes, but not necessarily for me or future poor folks coming by the church for help. When he heard about what I had done, my pastor was furious. Apparently we had a process in place for folks who visited churches in the town asking for help. They were told to go to the police station (can you imagine a place you would *not* want to go to if you were undocumented?) where they would be given money for a bus ticket to a town of their choice within a certain geographic area. My angry pastor irritatingly asked me, what would happen if every needy person in this town found out about this and started coming here for help? I didn't say anything, but thoughts of the New Testament church in the book of Acts crossed my mind.

I was amazed that a pastor would be so angry about his church members supporting a family who were obviously in need in such a vital way. Even more, I was stunned when I learned that the plan for caring for the poor was to ship them to the next town.

Most importantly though, while my church responded faithfully, neither they nor I ever stopped and asked why a boss of a local company was able to beat up his employees and face zero accountability. In addition, what would have happened if I had not painted the couple and their situation in such a sympathetic light? What would have happened if the couple with the child were a gay couple? What would have happened if I had told people the couple were undocumented, or to use the hateful vernacular, "illegal?"

Lastly, no one addressed the bizarre and frighteningly inhumane way we treated the poor through shipping them from our town to the next. My church responded lovingly, but we failed—I failed as a leader in the church—to address the symptoms of injustice or to break out of the deserving/undeserving framework that I used to give the family the resources they desperately needed. We who follow Jesus and are undeserved recipients of his unfailing love and grace use the deserving/undeserving framework to determine who is worthy of our love and who is not. Is there nothing in the church more blatantly contradictory to the heart of the gospel than this unquestioned practice of judging others' moral capacity to conclude who is eligible to receive gifts we might share—gifts we ascribe to the grace and goodness of God?

Lesson: Focusing on Fixing the Poor and Oppressed Alone Leaves Injustice in Place

In the end, though I had more compassion for the young family than my pastor did, we had the same problem: we assumed the powers in place were not in need of being addressed and the best way to address poverty and oppression was by reforming the poor and oppressed themselves. Thus, the problem of poverty and oppression was for us the same as it continues to be for far too many in local churches today; we reform the poor and oppressed while the people and structures responsible for the poverty and oppression remain untouched and in power. The real problem here of course is that when we leave structures in place that create poverty and oppression we will only exacerbate peoples' suffering.

The writer of Esther, like most of the writers of the scriptural texts, sees the problem of poverty as an unjust distribution of resources and the problem of oppression as an abuse of power. The question this first chapter challenges us with exists on societal, familial, individual and even ecclesial levels. If we are to live faithfully according to Scripture, then do we share the belief that the poor and oppressed are not the cause of their situation? Do we allow Scripture to shape our missiological engagement by working to address the structures of our society that create poverty and oppression and not merely by "fixing" the poor or oppressed themselves? Are we, in our local churches and not just through the institutional church bureaucracies, recognizing and then faithfully addressing an unjust distribution of resources and abuses by those in positions of power (in and out of the Church)?

I believe if we did allow Scripture to genuinely shape our views toward poverty and oppression, we would see a radical change in our federal and state policies, radical changes in our own lives and—perhaps even more—radical changes in the budgets and programming in our local churches and the ways we engage our communities. Perhaps the New Testament church wouldn't be such a diametrically alternative reality to our own if we lived this out. This is something to think on, and to act on.

Lessons Recapped:

- The framing of the book of Esther as well as the preponderance of Scripture is that the problem with poverty and the problem with oppression is not with the poor and oppressed themselves, but rather, with the unjust distribution of resources and an abuse of power, respectively.

- There is tremendous damage of classifying the poor as "deserving" or "undeserving" to the mission of the church as it is a cultural construct of the last 150 years and not based on the ways in which Scripture views the poor and the issue of poverty.

- Focusing on reforming the poor and oppressed without addressing the structures that cause the oppression and poverty leaves injustice intact and unchallenged.

Questions for Discussion:

1. In the initial discussion of the "players" of this story, is there a character you most admire? Scorn? Is there someone who relates to people or forces in your local context?

2. What are some passages in other parts of Scripture that agree with the premise that the problems of poverty and oppression are located in a problem of an unequal distribution of resources and a problem with the abuse of power? Do you find passages that differ?

3. Do you see in your local or national context examples of the responsibility of social ills being placed on the shoulders of the poor or oppressed? Share.

4. Does your local church have in place a policy of separating the "deserving" from the "undeserving?" What would it look like to not have those classifications in your missional work and outreach in your local church? What systems of injustice might you have to address if you refused to use the "deserving/undeserving" framework as you serve vulnerable populations in your local community?

Idea for Missional Engagement:

This exercise is one I have used before to get folks to think through This exercise is designed to address whether our service ministries in our churches are based on the deserving vs. undeserving model. On a sheet have your team list all of the ministries your church is involved in or supports. Under each one, list all of the rules or requirements that those who receive services must consent to in order to receive service. Some requirements might be ones that your ministry must accept from outside institutions, such as if your church serves as a warming shelter in the winter for the homeless. Make note of the rules that are imposed on your church from those that your church has created.

Before your group discusses the validity of the requirements get into groups of two or three and spend a couple of minutes in quiet reflection. Ask all participants to think through the internal thoughts and feelings of the people your church serves who are forced to comply with the rules you have listed. Then, in small groups, have each person speak from the perspective of those who receive services on how they feel about complying with such rules, using their inner thoughts and feelings.

For instance, if your church serves at a local immigration clinic and the clinic insists that families with children who get too loud must wait in another room or outside the building, then your group will speak from the inner thoughts and feelings of an immigrant mother with two small children.

Once your small group shares with one another then have all small groups share with the larger group. Talk about the validity of the rules or requirements from the perspective of those who are forced to comply with those rules. Ask yourselves if the rules are truly necessary or if there are ways that rules can be implemented that can still maintain the integrity of those who receive those services.

2

How to Get Away with Murder

If the first four chapters of Esther were a movie I am not sure it would be a good one to watch because there are parts of the story that simply go beyond the reaches of plausible imagination. For instance, nothing prepares the readers for the reaction Haman has in response to Mordecai's refusal to bow down. Talk about being a little over-sensitive! While we may have predicted that Haman would be angry due to Mordecai's lack of deference, what is not predictable is the extent to which Haman intends to punish Mordecai for his perceived lack of respect. Haman resolves to eradicate an entire race of people because of the actions of one man. Haman's actions are among the most heinous in all of Scripture.

Lesson: How to Advocate for Destruction and Not Get Dirty

One interesting aspect of Haman's anger is that Haman considered it "beneath him to lay hands on Mordecai alone" (3:5). The fact that he considered it "beneath him" to get into a physical altercation with Mordecai, but it was not "beneath him" to plan out a genocide of an entire race of people typifies Haman's new role as the second in command under the king. With Haman's rise in power comes an unwillingness to physically address Mordecai's insult because he now functions as an elite in the kingdom.

The elite of society are those small groups of people that are judged to be gifted with superior qualities and skills that allow them to occupy the highest roles in society; to run the government and business sectors especially. Plato believed that ruling elites needed to be free from physical labor so that they could engage in the much more significant work of philosophical contemplation and reasoning. More importantly—for Plato and often for many elites—everyone is born into their specific place in society, for this is how society is to efficiently work. It would be chaos for Plato if philosophers were made to do unskilled labor and brick layers were asked to contemplate the meaning of life.[1] Accordingly, Mordecai's refusal to bow seems treasonous for Haman because it means that an ordinary Jew has now assumed a position of equality with Haman. Mordecai's action, whether intentioned or not, takes on revolutionary meaning in the eyes of those in power.

Haman feels compelled to respond to Mordecai's insurrectionary action but his lofty status defines his role, his actions. Though Haman shuns a fistfight because the outward appearance of violence is beneath him, Haman is intent, no matter his position, to destructively utilize his access to resources in order to cut off others' already restricted access to resources. Herein lies an example of advocacy that we will do well to remember, though Haman's advocacy is for an evil outcome. Henceforth, we will call this *destructive advocacy*. Though Haman opts for a less outwardly violent response to Mordecai's revolutionary act, Haman's actions will be absolutely brutal in their impact.

Lesson: Committing Genocide Is Not as Hard as You Think

With his goal to eradicate the Jews in mind, Haman picks an opportune moment to approach King Ahasuerus and launch his plan. His manipulation of the king is masterful. This part of the

---

1. Justice, for Plato, "is to perform one's own task and not to meddle with that of others." Solomon and Murphy, *What Is Justice?*, 35. Solomon and Murphy provide excellent insight into Plato's view toward justice.

story illustrates of how entire groups of people can be dehumanized so subtly, but yet so cunningly. In order to slaughter all the
Jews in the kingdom Haman must make his personal grievance
more general for he cannot be seen to be holding a grudge. He
has to impersonalize it. He must persuade the king that if the Jews
remain they will threaten the very well-being of King Ahasuerus
and the entire Persian kingdom.

He begins his argument with a statement of relative truth.
"There is a certain people scattered and separated among the peoples in all the provinces of your kingdom" (3:8). Haman knows he
cannot just walk up to the King and ask him to commit genocide
against the Jews. He must be more subtle and build up to his request. He smartly begins where his listener is and with a statement
that anyone would agree with so he can earn the king's trust before
he moves on to his more diabolical intentions. The Jews are indeed
spread throughout the kingdom.

Haman then begins to swerve from truthfulness as he says,
"they do not keep the king's laws" (3:8). This is an entirely merit-
less statement. Though it is true that the Jews have their own laws
which they keep, this does not prevent them from living law-abid-
ing lives under Persian rule. Just look at Mordecai's earlier example
when he uncovers a plot to assassinate the King. It is Mordecai's
obedience to the laws that saves the king's life. Haman's insinua-
tion is little more than a thinly veiled attack on the ethnicity and
religion of Mordecai and his people.

More than anything, we see here that Haman is not interested
in the specific human stories that show the contributions of Jews to
real life in the Persian kingdom, such as Mordecai saving the life of
the king. He must keep his references to the Jewish people impersonal so that he can paint as dark a picture as possible. Committing evil against a people is much easier when the people who are
being targeted remain faceless and nameless. The more personal
they are the more difficult it is to order their extinction. Haman
must dehumanize the Jews and create an image of the Jews as an
enemy; as inhuman. In other words, he must lie.

Now Haman moves in for the kill, "so that it is not appropriate for the king to tolerate them." Notice he has still not said that the king needs to kill them. He allows the king to remain something of a passive spectator. The Jews should just "not be tolerated." Killing someone entails action and is often done on a personal level. There are often emotions that accompany the act of killing someone. But Haman has so dehumanized the Jews that emotions are not needed. The Jews should just not be allowed to exist.

So, Haman proceeds to make his primary request of the king, which I will include in full:

> If it pleases the king, let a decree be issued for their destruction, and I will pay ten thousand talents of silver into the hands of those who have charge of the king's business so that they may put it into the king's treasuries. (3:9)

Even now, when Haman finally makes his request of the king he never asks the king to commit any overt action. He doesn't ask that the king write a decree, but rather, just that a decree be issued. It is almost as if the decree will write itself and walk out into the kingdom on its own to be proclaimed. Evil becomes easy to engage in when it doesn't require the accessory to lift a finger in assistance. The less one has to do the easier complicity will be.

But Haman also wants the king to benefit from the eradication of the "Jewish problem" so he offers a bribe. Again, in the interests of clearing the king from any culpability or linkage to this horrible crime, the money will never touch the king's person. The money will be put into the "hands of those who have charge of the king's business." Haman makes sure that the king will have zero liability of the crime being committed while reaping all of the benefits. And the king, like all elites, understands the need for both subtlety and deniability. In response, "the king took his signet ring from his hand and gave it to Haman" (3:10). The king, without writing a single instruction or uttering one direct command, had authored the genocide of the Jews by signifying his approval through the passing of his ring, the symbol of his authority, to Haman.

Lesson: The Subtlety of Evil and the Danger of "Purity"

This is how evil is done. Evil is done subtly with a complete lack of culpability for those highest in positions of power. The easy slide into the participation of evil without any direct linkage to the actual evil acts committed provides the necessary cover for those with the highest of titles. Evil is easily done when it is done effortlessly, when it can become systematized and the evil act itself is reduced to a routine institutional matter of paperwork without public scrutiny.

What Haman embarks on through the destructive utilization of power to influence the king is what Miroslav Volf calls the "politics of purity." In cases where there have been great massacres of people based on their race or ethnicity—what came to be called ethnic cleansing in the 1990s when Volf was writing—the drive behind those violent occurrences has been to "go back to the pristine purity of our linguistic, religious or cultural past, shake away the dirt of otherness . . . plurality and heterogeneity must give way to homogeneity and unity. One people, one culture, one language, one book, one goal."[2] The politics of purity often resounds popular themes in political campaigns when the call is sounded to "take our country back" or "make America great again" as it once was in times gone by when "those people" weren't around to create the social distress we blame them for now. But hidden beneath these themes are the lurking sins of ethnic hatred and the desire for renewed exclusive supremacy of the dominant culture. This is the politics of purity, older than Scripture itself, but always present with us.

Care Study of Evil: Mass Incarceration

Though we see the "politics of purity" throughout world history, those in the U.S. have our own examples. The discovery of the Americas by Europeans saw the near obliteration of indigenous peoples, including some entire tribes wiped out through disease

2. Volf, *Exclusion & Embrace*, 74.

or wars. Land was stolen, treaties were made and then broken shortly thereafter. One group of people who have felt the sting of generations of racism and oppression are African Americans. The building of a national economy and the transformation of a small country into an international trading power happened on the backs of mostly African slaves shipped to this country (and others) like cargo for the sole purpose of making whites affluent. It is not coincidental that remnants of the Platonic philosophy we discussed earlier in this chapter should frame the attitudes of those who benefitted from the system of slavery in the United States. The southern elites were those who defended not only the practice of slavery, but also its philosophical and theological underpinnings as the elites believed "racial slavery was the labor system most conducive to the elevation of the intellect, since it protected some men from the allurements of greed and gave leisure to the master class that could cultivate 'mental improvements and refinement of manners.'"[3]

In time, slavery was abolished, but a new system of laws and social regulations called "Jim Crow" was established and upheld as legally binding by the Supreme Court decision in the 1896 case, Plessy vs. Ferguson. "Separate but equal" became the legal standard for how African Americans were mistreated. C. Vann Woodward points out that the installation of the Jim Crow laws were gradual, beginning in the compromise of 1877, which handed Rutherford B. Hayes the presidency and the South their "independence" from the presence of northern troops. Thus, African Americans were disenfranchised and exploited for generations into the twentieth century through a system of "Jim Crow" laws which made segregation legal.[4]

Though there arose, of course, the modern civil rights movement which removed much of this kind of systemic racism and the legal justification for Jim Crow segregation, according to Michelle Alexander there has arisen a new system of "Jim Crow" laws revolving around the criminal justice system. Alexander maintains

3. Davis, *Inhuman Bondage*, 188.
4. Woodward, *Strange Career of Jim Crow*, 6–7.

that "today it is perfectly legal to discriminate against criminals in nearly all of the ways that it was once legal to discriminate against African Americans."[5] Alexander points out that the war on drugs waged by every administration, both Democratic and Republican since it was started by President Nixon, has been devastating to the African American community. Though whites use and sell drugs at higher rates than do people of color, particularly African Americans, it is people of color who are incarcerated at dramatically higher rates. During the era of the war on drugs the number of those incarcerated has exploded from 300,000 to more than 2 million as of this writing. Furthermore, "in some states black men have been admitted to prison on drug charges at rates twenty to fifty times greater than those of white men. And in major cities wracked by the drug war, as many as 80 percent of young African American men now have criminal records and are thus subject to legalized discrimination for the rest of their lives."[6]

The collateral consequences of mass incarceration[7] includes, in some states, lifelong political disenfranchisement. Some length of political disenfranchisement impacts over 1.4 million African American males, or 13 percent of the adult African American population.[8] Excluding people who have served time in prison from their right to vote has had tremendous political impact. It has been estimated that "disenfranchisement policies have affected the outcome of seven U.S. Senate races from 1970, when the war on drugs began to 1998 . . . In each case the Democratic candidate would have won rather than the Republican victor. Projecting the impact of these races over time leads them to conclude that disenfranchisement prevented democratic control of the Senate from 1986 to 2000."[9]

5. Alexander, *New Jim Crow*, 2.

6. Ibid., 6–7.

7. The term "mass incarceration," as defined by Michelle Alexander, means "the larger web, rules, policies, and customs that control those labeled criminals both in and out of prison." Ibid., 13.

8. Mauer and Chesney-Lind, *Invisible Punishment*, 4.

9. Ibid., 53.

But excluding the voices of returning citizens isn't the only impact mass incarceration has on people of color. Though the war on drugs has fictionally been waged to lower the use and dependence on drugs, the policies adopted as a result of this war have had a tragically adverse effect. There is widespread agreement that treatment is more effective and less expensive than harsh punishment-oriented responses to drug use. However, the political response has consistently been to punish people who often are committing crimes to support an addiction with mandatory minimum sentences rather than with treatment. One way we do this is by denying people with drug-related felonies access to crucial social services like Temporary Assistance for Needy Families (TANF) benefits. "Thus, a person convicted of armed robbery can qualify for TANF assistance after completing a sentence, but someone with a single felony conviction for drug possession cannot."[10] Furthermore, we have, for some reason, made access to drug treatment for people currently incarcerated more difficult to attain and therefore, the availability of drug treatment for those suffering from addiction has actually been on the decline in recent years.[11]

The impact of the criminal justice system on the African American community has been devastating. Alexander's contention is that this is not an accident; this has been intentional. It is not only in the sentencing of people of color to extraordinarily long sentences—much longer than given to whites for the same offenses committed—it is also in the lifelong denial of rights. "Once released, former prisoners enter a hidden underworld of legalized discrimination and permanent social exclusion. They are members of America's new undercaste."[12]

Miroslav Volf suggests that the "practice of exclusion," such as the impact of the criminal justice system on the African American community that Michelle Alexander describes, goes hand in hand with the "language of exclusion," something we see evident in Haman's argument to the king about the need to no longer "tolerate"

10. Ibid., 41.
11. Ibid., 38–39.
12. Alexander, *New Jim Crow*, 13.

the Jews.[13] Volf also states that "some of the most brutal acts of exclusion depend on hatred, and if the common history of persons and communities does not contain enough reasons to hate, masters of exclusion will rewrite the histories and fabricate injuries in order to manufacture hatreds."[14] This is exactly what we saw with Haman, who appears to be one of Volf's "masters of exclusion" as he blatantly lied to the king about the lawlessness of the Jews. The dehumanization of the Jews which led to the adoption of policies that attempt to eradicate their race (orchestrated by Haman) has been repeated throughout history by people in power against racial and ethnic groups who are marginalized and exploited. This is certainly what we have seen over the last forty plus years in the construct of mass incarceration as political elites have cast their support for harsh punishments using half-truths and blatant lies. Calling black urban youth "super-predators" in the early nineties to pass inhumane laws against our youth, or fearing the rise of an epidemic of "crack babies" (also demonizing urban and mostly black families) are unnerving examples of Volf's "language of exclusion." The language of exclusion and the politics of purity have maintained devastating results for generations of African Americans who suffer from mass incarceration.

Lesson: Genocide and Injustices Are Rooted in Racism

Like the sin of mass incarceration being rooted in structural racism, Haman too commits a great sin that is rooted in racism. The question I have constantly asked myself as I read this story in recent years is why would he expend so much of his own political capital to annihilate a group of people who have done virtually nothing to offend him (besides Mordecai's one "offense")? What is the payoff for Haman? I must admit this is similar to asking why we in the United States have maintained the system of slavery that became Jim Crow segregation and now goes by the name of

13. Volf, *Exclusion & Embrace*, 76–77.
14. Ibid., 77.

mass incarceration viable for so long. The answer is both sad and all too obvious. When the king's authority is passed onto Haman through the king's ring the writer identifies for the readers who Haman is. It reads, "Haman, son of Hammedatha the Agagite, the enemy of the Jews" (3:10).

Agag was once king of Amalekites who attacked Israel during the years they wandered in the wilderness. The Amalekites suffered defeat from the Israelites led by Joshua, while Moses watched. Israel's God takes particular offense with the Amalekites and promises wars "from generation to generation" (Exod 17:8–16). This brief history helps to form the basis for Haman's anti-Semitism. Thus, Haman plans to exterminate the Jews because he hates the Jews. And Haman hates the Jews because he was raised to hate the Jews from his father and the generations before him. If Haman had not risen to the powerful place he occupied at that time in the government he certainly would have acted on his hatred against the Jewish people in another way. Haman was intent, no matter his position, to destructively utilize his access to resources in order to cut off others' already restricted access to resources.

This is what we earlier defined as destructive advocacy. As Haman's hatred for the Jews led him to devise such a horrific plan that he executed perfectly using his position of power, so too is the current system of mass incarceration rooted in generational racism. As Michelle Alexander persuasively argues, mass incarceration is not accidental. Haman's racist hatred would have fueled his destructive advocacy no matter his political position.

It seems ludicrous that Haman could be so angry that he seeks to eradicate all of the Jews in the kingdom until we understand that Haman's rage against the Jews had been there all along. Haman's hatred passed down to him from his father along with his unprecedented access to power made him a terrifying threat to the Jews. Likewise, entrenched societal racism and the beginning of a campaign in the early 1970s aimed at eliminating drug usage through harsh penalties has birthed a criminal justice system that is inherently racist and devastating to the African American community.

Though Haman's plans are thwarted in the end we are left with the sobering reminder that the combination of systemic racism and unchecked power makes for devastating results. We see this not just in the pages of Scripture or history books, but in the injustices that so many people face today in the United States.

Lessons Recapped:

- Destructive advocacy is to destructively utilize one's access to resources in order to cut off others' already restricted access to resources.

- Committing genocide is not as hard as you think; for it requires making the targets of your evil intentions as impersonal as possible, to dehumanize them through lies and careful innuendos, while providing zero liability for those in power to take actions against them.

- The subtlety of evil and the danger of "purity" is pervasive throughout history and shows how evil is committed with little culpability for people in positions of power.

- Genocide, like so many societal injustices, is rooted in racism and racism wedded with power is devastating for the impacted community.

Questions for Discussion:

1. Can you think of comparable examples of injustices occurring in the world today or in history compared to what Esther and Mordecai were facing? What are they?

2. If destructive advocacy is to destructively utilize one's access to resources in order to cut off others' already restricted access to resources, are there examples you see today where destructive advocacy is taking place against specific impacted communities of people? Who are advocating for the kind of

destruction you have identified? Is there anything in your local context that you can point to?

3. Are there groups in your local context who are dehumanized through lies and innuendos in the same way done against the Jews in this story? How has this dehumanization led to their mistreatment?

4. Underlying the dangers of ethnic cleansing and the call for national purity is the sin of racism. This can be a difficult subject to talk openly about without becoming unnecessarily accusatory or overly defensive. With our hearts tender and open, can you look at the injustices in your local context and see if there is racism lurking underneath? Again, with tender and open hearts, is there a way in which you benefit or a way in which you are hurt by any racism that may exist?

Idea for Missional Engagement:

In 2013 I worked with a media company called Brave New Films to create a short film (approximately twenty-two minutes long) about mass incarceration, told from the perspective of someone who helped perpetuate mass incarceration—an Assistant Attorney General for the state of Tennessee.

When the film was released there were hundreds of showings throughout the United States. It is a powerful film that shows the devastating impact of mass incarceration not only on those imprisoned, but on those who are part of the system as well.

I encourage you to view this together. The film is now on Youtube: https://www.youtube.com/watch?v=dQpQlqN8EYo.

Film Discussion Questions:

- What caused this change in Preston to go from celebrating his role of Assistant Attorney General to wanting to have nothing to do with it?

- When Preston found out he was responsible for keeping Cyntoia incarcerated he sought forgiveness from her. Was he right to seek forgiveness? Why or why not? What would you have done in his situation?

- Did Cyntoia deserve her sentence? Why or why not? Would a different response to her crime have better served the common good?

- What does Preston's story reveal about the problems in the U.S. criminal justice system?

- What are some of the policies that our nation should adopt to improve our criminal justice system? How can we reduce mass incarceration while maintaining public safety?

- What can you personally do about mass incarceration that you're not doing? What's your responsibility to those who are in prison?

3

Righteousness in the Light of Day

The confrontation between Haman and Mordecai is a classic conflict between the bad guy who designs sinister plans to destroy the world (or part of it anyway) and the good guys who, with little access to resources, find creative ways to save the world. In the last chapter we looked at Haman; in comparison, now we will examine Mordecai, one our valiant protagonists. Whereas Haman is manipulative and acts behind closed doors to destructively utilize his access to resources in order to cut off others' already restricted access to resources, Mordecai is the honest and straightforward type with the highest of aspirations and the purest of intentions. Mordecai brings to light the assassination attempt against the king and openly refuses to bow down in homage to Haman. Later, upon the reading of the edict to all the provinces in the kingdom of the impending genocide of the Jews, it is Mordecai who decides that he will not go quietly into that good night. Haman concocted in private, with coded language and bureaucratic finesse; Mordecai will now openly express his grief for the world to see. Mordecai will help shine a bright spotlight on what Haman deceitfully planned in the dark.

Lesson: Public Witness Carries both Spiritual and Political Implications

As we saw earlier, Mordecai's open refusal to bow down before Haman can be seen as an act of insurrection. Again, the text does not exactly say why Mordecai refused to bow, but if it was indeed out of obedience to worship no other gods besides Yahweh (which I believe it is), then Mordecai's act of disobedience is also an act of worship. Thus, Mordecai's actions carry both spiritual and political implications. His actions make the powerful message of not only what he is against politically (the demand of hero-worship from a political leader), but also what he is for spiritually (the public witness of fidelity to God).

All too often the term "politics" takes on a negative connotation because it is so often associated with fights between two sides vying for power, whether that takes place in Washington DC, state capitols, or in denominational offices. Politics is something we want nothing to do with. But political engagement, as shown through Mordecai's open refusal to bow before Haman, is not limited to partisan campaigns or endless bickering by two entrenched sides. Political engagement is not even limited to advocating for legislation at the state or federal level (though that is of great importance). Limiting political activity to these kinds of actions misses out on the transformative elements of political engagement; times when peoples' lives are bettered and society is transformed.

Political advocacy often takes place in what we see as the most mundane actions such as helping citizens returning from years of incarceration reintegrate back into their home communities, registering new voters in lower-income communities, or dispelling misinformation among our friends, families, or fellow church members that demonizes immigrants and refugees. All of this and more are part of what I am calling political advocacy. However, because many of us are part of churches where the spiritual and the political have been falsely bifurcated we are often unaware that those actions carry tremendous political meaning.

The split between the political and spiritual that is all too evident in our churches does not have a biblical basis. We need only look at his call to mission in Luke's gospel where he announces the beginning of his ministry. He quotes from Isaiah, claiming he has been called to "preach good news to the poor . . . proclaim release to the captives, and recovery of sight to the blind, [and] to let the oppressed go free" (4:18). The message Jesus came not only to preach, but to embody in his life and ministry, carried enormous political implications, particularly for the poor and oppressed. Jesus was not just a starry-eyed dreamer content to preach abstract messages of hope of another world while he spent his time in constant prayerful solitude. Jesus' actions and teachings were innately social and therefore inherently political as they so often challenged the way people interacted with others; both those in positions of power and those who were crushed by injustice. As followers of Jesus we are called to manifest his life, ministry, and teachings in our lives, realizing that there will be radical implications within the political realm. Jesus didn't come so that we can merely sing praise songs. He came to bring about a social, economic, spiritual and yes, political revolution.

In the story of Esther, some of the more prominent actions that involve political advocacy include:

- Mordecai reporting the plot he overheard at the city gate to assassinate the king;

- Haman manipulating the king to issue the edict condemning all Jews to their death;

- Mordecai refusing to bow down before Haman;

- Mordecai grieving in front of the city gate upon hearing the edict announcing the ensuing genocide;

- Mordecai organizing all of the Jews in Susa to pray and fast for Esther for three days before she approaches the king; and

- Esther's approach to the king to plead for the lives of her people.

All of these listed above are clearly political actions. Because the political is so intertwined in all that we do as a civil society, and because advocacy occurs when we work for the benefit of a person or group that is being mistreated or excluded in some way, I would like to offer a new definition of political advocacy from a missiological perspective. In this framework, *redemptive advocacy* is to use one's access to resources to *gain* such access for those whose access has been denied. Notice that this is the exact opposite of what we saw Haman doing in the last chapter, though what he did, as listed above, also constitutes political advocacy. While Haman engaged in the destructive use of his access to resources in order to cut off others' already restricted access to resources (what we call destructive advocacy), Mordecai and Esther, on the other hand, redemptively use their access to resources to gain such access for those whose access has been denied (what we call redemptive advocacy).

Haman destructively advocated for himself and acted out of the racist hatred passed down from his father by attempting to eliminate any access for the Jews. Esther redemptively advocated for the safety of her people when she sacrificially utilized her access to the king to gain life for her people. And even before this, Mordecai redemptively advocated for his people after the edict had been read by utilizing his access to Esther to urge her to take action on behalf of her people. The book of Esther gives great evidence of how the spiritual and the political can and do interact. This intentional interaction brings about tremendous change. This is why advocacy should be seen and practiced by local churches as both a spiritual discipline and a missiological practice.

I remember early on in the Obama administration there was some concern that the issue of mass incarceration was not being placed as a priority within the Administration. Of course, early on in the Administration the fight for universal health care reform and a number of other issues were taking center stage, but as advocates we knew the criminal justice system was only growing in its devastating impact on local communities and families each day, so time was of the essence to raise this as a priority for the White House.

There had been numerous meetings with White House staffers and the Department of Justice citing the importance and need for criminal justice reform, with advocacy organizations always referring to the cost savings that comes from diverting people away from long prison sentences and to things like substance abuse treatment for those whose crimes are low-level drug offenses. The White House staff we met with all agreed with our reasoning, but something more was needed to move them toward action. So, we flew in faith leaders from across the United States, with some having been formerly incarcerated themselves, so that they could meet with Administration staff and could testify to the impact that mass incarceration was having on the people in their congregations and communities.

At the meeting, they shared about the amazing ministries they were part of and told stories of the devastation of mass incarceration while pointing to some specific policies that directly impacted their lives and their communities. It was a powerful meeting to be in. The message to the White House and Department of Justice staff at the end was simple: "we are doing all we can to care for people directly impacted by mass incarceration, but we can't solve it by ourselves. You can and must help us."

While things did not start to happen overnight—they almost never do, by the way—there was movement. I could sense a greater receptivity on the part of White House staff to requests that the faith community was making. Our faith coalition was often pointed to by Administration staffers as a coalition to model because of the theological and political diversity of our members and our engagement with the grassroots. Not surprisingly, it was early in President Obama's second term that he began to make ending mass incarceration a priority. Our strategy for making criminal justice reform more of a priority for the Administration was a simple one (and they usually are): make the stories of those directly impacted heard by people in positions of power. The more evident our efforts are the more likely greater attention will be placed on the injustice and its impact on vulnerable people.

Evil works exactly in the opposite way. The less people are able to see how deceitfulness is planned out and accomplished the more effective the injustice is. As the curtain in the book of Esther is drawn on the evil committed by Haman and the king at the end of chapter 3 we see their contentment in the midst of the terror they have sown.

> Letters were sent by couriers to all the king's provinces, giving orders to destroy, to kill, and to annihilate all Jews, young and old, women and children, in one day, the thirteenth day of the twelfth month, which is the month of Adar, and to plunder their goods. A copy of the document was to be issued as a decree in every province by proclamation, calling on all the peoples to be ready for that day. The couriers went quickly by order of the king, and the decree was issued in the citadel of Susa. The King and Haman sat down to drink; but the city of Susa was thrown into confusion (3:13–15).

The image of the final verse here is striking. The entire city of Susa, which was the primary of four ancient Persian capitals,[1] was thrown into confusion at the reading of this unprecedented announcement. It wasn't just the Jews. All of Susa was shaken as they learned that an entire race was to be murdered and their property confiscated while Haman and the king relax with a nice, tall glass of lemonade (at least that's what I picture!). Their utter detachment from the evil they have set in motion cannot be illustrated any better.

Lesson: Self-Interest Is a Step toward Change

Though the text does not comment on this, I cannot help but wonder if the confusion that resulted in Susa was seen as a positive thing in Mordecai's thinking. It certainly would have been devastating if life went on like business as usual when the public heard the plans to exterminate the Jews. The confusion shows that the people of Susa were in relationship with those directly impacted by the planned genocide. This shows in part why our efforts to publicize injustices can make our advocacy more effective; the more people are exposed to injustice and in particular, exposed to someone who will be directly impacted by the injustice, the more they will be likely to act in their defense.

1. Fox, *Character and Ideology*, 15.

36

Though all of us often profess our allegiance to the highest moral values that hopefully guide us, our impulses are most often focused on our own welfare. This seems only natural. However, focusing on our own interests does not have to be opposed to being focused on the interests of others.

The concept of self-interest is enormously important in creating change. The Midwest Academy, which trains community organizers, holds that people will decide to participate in movements for social change because that change benefits them and gives them meaning. Self-interest is not just centered in selfishness. Instead, self-interest often means discovering one's identity in deeper relationships among others.[2] This definition shows us that our interests are actually inexplicably intertwined with those who are around us, so as we are immersed in relationships with those directly impacted by injustice our self-interest will more authentically reflect the interests of those directly impacted by that injustice.

Let me offer an example of how this has worked in the past. In December of 2005 the U.S. House of Representatives passed harsh legislation (H.R. 4437) aimed at punishing undocumented immigrants and further militarizing the southern border. There were a number of troubling provisions, but the one that received the highest concern among faith communities made it an aggravated felony for anyone who provided certain means of support for undocumented immigrants. For instance, there were stiff penalties for someone caught providing transportation for undocumented immigrants. Faith communities were outraged because it meant that anyone driving a group of undocumented children to the church for Vacation Bible School would result in the arrest and detainment of everyone in the van. This ill-conceived legislation passed by the House accomplished what hadn't been occurring prior to 2005; it made the faith community take to the streets in protest, following the lead of immigrant communities.

The response to this draconian legislation was immediate and intense. Tens of thousands of immigrants poured into the streets

2. Bobo, et al., *Organizing for Social Change*, 6.

in cities throughout the United States as people refused to cower in fear. Included in these marches and protests were many clergy and laity who, for the first time, became actively engaged in public protest because they were so outraged at the provisions contained in the law. Like the people of Susa, many cities and towns (especially the houses of worship in those cities and towns) were thrown into confusion at the announcement of the House-passed legislation. I received many emails from United Methodists who were appalled at what had passed out of the House of Representatives and they wanted to know how they could be involved to stop it. Much of the church-based organizing that has become so prevalent in recent years among United Methodists and other faith groups began with that dreadful piece of legislation in 2005–2006. But it required that the interests of the faith communities had to be impacted along with the immigrants they were in relationship with.

Lesson: Evil Is Achieved through Detachment from Those Directly Impacted

While there certainly are exceptions, systemic evil thrives where those directly impacted are separated from those who are directly or indirectly culpable for the evil. As we will see with Esther and Mordecai—the evil is only pushed back when those directly impacted by injustice lead the movement for justice, and then are joined by those who have access to resources to address the injustice, and the two groups' self-interests become conjoined. This is precisely what happened in 2006 between faith communities and immigrant communities to beat back the horrible legislation passed in the House of Representatives.

The pivotal fourth chapter in Esther opens with Mordecai and other Jews in the kingdom realizing their fate at the reading of the edicts in every province of the kingdom. Though the text never suggests there was any kind of organized response by the Jewish people to the announcement of the edict, the response to this news was similar to Mordecai's everywhere it was read. There was widespread public mourning (4:3). Mordecai and the other

Jews throughout the kingdom tore their clothes, "put on sackcloth and ashes, and went through the city, wailing with a loud and bitter cry" (4:1). Tearing one's clothes, putting on sackcloth and ashes, and wailing from the grief of hearing such terrible news is recorded in other passages of Scriptures and thus was a common response to tragedy.[3]

However, Mordecai takes this common cultural response and gives it intentionality and political meaning so that it can be understood as a protest against their impending doom. Mordecai could have easily gone into hiding out of great sorrow, or he could have wailed loudly in a place where only he and his people could hear, which would be a natural impulse for someone to want to be around others who share their sense of pain. Though natural, responses like these would not have led to a public outcry or effective and concerted action. Instead, Mordecai, even in the midst of his grief, is deliberately planning his response to stop the pending holocaust of his people.

Mordecai goes to a strategic place to publicly mourn. "He went up to the entrance of the king's gate."[4] The city gate functioned as a meeting place where important events and civic business was

3. Some of the other passages include Gen 37:29; 1 Sam 4:12; 2 Sam 1:2; 3:31; 13:19; 1 Kgs 20:31; 2 Kgs 6:30; Job 1:20.

4. The city gates occupied a significant place in Scripture as central meeting places where important business was conducted. Some instances to note include:

- In Genesis 19:1 Lot, the nephew of Abraham, met the two angels of the Lord at the gate of Sodom and then welcomed them to his house.

- In Genesis 22:17, in response to Abraham's willingness to sacrifice his son Isaac, an angel of the Lord promises blessings upon Abraham and his descendants, including the promise that his "offspring shall possess the gate of their enemies." Thus, taking the city gate from one's enemy ensures that you have defeated your enemy's city.

- Decisions of judgment were often made at city gates as shown in Deuteronomy 21:18.

- King David stood at the city gate in 2 Samuel 18:4 to inspect his troops as they left the city for battle and then returned to the gate when the troops returned in victory, though David met them in mourning for the death of his son, Absalom (2 Sam 19:8).

conducted. In the book of Esther, Mordecai was at the city gate twice before: when he uncovered the plot to assassinate the king and when he refused to bow down before Haman. Therefore, Mordecai goes to this significant place so that his grief can be turned into a protest in order to stop the injustice. Mordecai's mourning is both an act of protest—evidence of the political—and an emotional outcry for salvation—evidence of sincere worship.

Of course, I do not liken myself to experiencing anything similar to what Mordecai must have been experiencing, but I do resonate how engaging in protest and civil disobedience can be worshipful. On President's Day, February 17, 2014, I joined a group of undocumented immigrants and faith leaders as we engaged in civil disobedience in front of the White House to protest the two millionth deportation during President Obama's administration. We wanted to put an end to mass deportations that were literally terrorizing immigrant communities.

We had two audiences in mind for our action. We of course wanted to move the heart of President Obama to put an end to this horrible policy, but we also hoped to pierce the hearts of those in the church who had chosen to sit idly by, to watch immigrant families be torn apart by raids and indefinite detention and who had yet to lift a finger to stop it. Daily, immigrants lived in fear that at any time and in any place they or their loved ones might be indefinitely detained and possibly deported, with no word to any of their loved ones left wondering where they had gone. We wanted to mobilize communities of faith to do more than just write empty statements from bureaucratic offices that were falling on political deaf ears. That had gotten us exactly nowhere.

It was all too easy for faith leaders and national offices to stand behind a microphone at a press conference or a rally, or to make eloquent statements proclaiming their outrage. But far too few were willing to stand and refuse to move in front of the White House and demand an end to the brutal treatment of our immigrant sisters and brothers. Too many faith leaders and national faith offices seemed more concerned about maintaining access to the power located in the White House rather than prophetically speaking against injustice perpetrated by an Administration over-reliant on deportations.

The reason for the deportations was what sickened us and finally moved us to engage in civil disobedience. It had nothing to do with the rhetoric coming out of the White House—that they were deporting hardened criminals and those who posed genuine threats to public safety. We knew that many of those who had been deported were threats to no one. Most in fact were hard-working, contributing members of local communities and congregations. The real reason for the two million deportations was entirely political, no matter the empty rhetoric.

So, our small group stood in front of the White House and refused to move when asked to do so by the Capitol Park police. The police knew we were engaging in a public protest, but what we intentionally failed to tell them was that, in an attempt to share in the struggles of our immigrant sisters and brothers who are arrested and have no official identification, we had left our driver's licenses with those not getting arrested. We actually had a number of undocumented immigrants getting arrested with us and we did not want to leave them in jail when those of us who had identification were released solely because we had been born here and did not have to leave our country of origin in order to try to earn enough money to feed our families. Ours was a political protest.

But it was also so much more for those who were arrested. I remember distinctly the feeling of standing in front of the White House while we prayed and sang and read Scripture. As the leader of the demonstration I was trying to keep my mind fixed on the logistics. I was also nervous about how the police would react when we told them that none of us had IDs. But I was swept along with the songs we sang, the Scriptures being read, and with the heartfelt prayers we lifted up to ask for an end to state-sponsored terror. It truly was a heavenly moment and I could sense the presence of the Holy Spirit being with us.

The actual arrest was supposed to take a couple of hours at the most, but it lasted well into the night. Our lack of IDs made life very difficult for the police and they were not happy. I do not blame them one bit. We chose to enter jail together and we would not leave until all of us left together—which we ultimately did—though it took considerably longer than we had planned.

Sadly, the deportations did not end the next day as we hoped. But the political tide had begun to shift and the Administration was on the defensive about the impact their policies had on immigrant families and entire local communities, from then on. The political conversation had been moved.

We also literally shamed other faith leaders into joining us for the next act of civil disobedience, which occurred just five months later. That action was shortly followed by President Obama's expansion of his earlier action which granted temporary legal status to a group of DREAMers and to some of their family members. Our political act of protest was powerful because it was also worshipful.

Lesson: Because Advocacy Is Both Political and Worshipful

Our act of civil disobedience in front of the White House also highlighted the fact that the prophetic task is not reserved for a few "big names" with impressive titles, but is open to all. It is, in fact, imperative for all. We just have to be willing to listen to our immigrant sisters and brothers, hear the devastation in the stories they tell us, and be willing to risk our safety to gain safety alongside them. Mordecai was a man of no tremendous name or title, but he intentionally and strategically made his protest public so that his anguish would be conveyed to touch the hearts of those in positions of power, namely Queen Esther. Justice, throughout the pages of Scripture and down through history, always seems to come through the most unexpected of vehicles; through the lives of those who are not born into places or positions of influence or power.

This is an important lesson for followers of Jesus who seem too focused on waiting for the hierarchy of the church, those with titles and status positions to step out in front and lead. I cannot count how many times I have talked with local clergy and laity who are hesitant to step out because they are waiting for their Bishop or someone with some similar title to make advocacy and organizing for justice a priority. How blind and obstinate we are! Have we not read where the anointing of the Holy Spirit falls on the son of a carpenter to preach good news to the poor, release to the captives and freedom to the oppressed? God is not waiting for your diocese or conference, your bishop or even your pastor to tell you to advocate and organize for justice. Jesus has already done so!

So, let us be reminded of the power of God who can take a baby from an obscure town in the Middle East and bring, through his life and death, liberation to the world. Perhaps God will take an unknown local church from an obscure part of the world to bring about justice for the people in your community? Perhaps you and your community are in such a place for such a time as this?

Out in the open, for the world to see. This is how righteousness works.

Lessons Recapped:

- Our public witness carries both spiritual and political implications and the two cannot and should not be separated.

- Self-interest means self among others. We participate in the process of creating change as we are immersed in relationships among those directly impacted by injustice because it mobilizes people around common cause and shared passion.

- Evil is achieved through detachment from those directly impacted while righteousness is achieved through incarnation among those directly impacted.

- Because advocacy for justice is both worshipful and political we are all called to engage in it and not to wait for those with titles or status positions to give us permission. Permission has already been granted for everyone and not just for a select few!

Questions for Discussion:

1. Do you believe that engagement in political advocacy and public witness can be missional and worshipful? Why or why not? Have you experienced the presence of God through advocacy or public witness?

2. Do you think one's self-interest can be connected to the interests of others or will there always be irreparable conflict? What is required for one's self-interest to be aligned with the interests of others?

3. Do you have examples where secondary issues sidetracked you from the primary goal? Is this a problem for local churches when addressing issues of injustice? Why or why not?

4. Do you believe titles or statuses get in the way for those in the local church working for justice? Can you share any examples as to whether you have seen this happen or not?

Idea for Missional Engagement:

Rent or buy the documentary *Eyes on the Prize*. As a group, watch one or two (or all) of the episodes. As you watch, each person make a list of what is being done—the events that occur, the public witness actions made in response to those events, etc. Make a list of the public witness events organized by the protagonists and if evident, make a similar list of what was done by the antagonists.

Then compare the lists and discuss.

- What kind of actions and events did the protagonists engage in?

- What kind of actions and events did the antagonists engage in?

- What were the effects of the actions and events by the protagonists? Did they raise awareness? Did they add numbers to their cause?

- What can we take from their example and apply it to our own context?

For those who want to add more books that cover the historical importance of organizing to your reading list, I strongly encourage you to read *Local People*, by John Dittmer, and *I've Got the Light of Freedom*, by Charles Payne. Both are excellent.

4

The Captivity of Detachment

I remember the day that I decided I would no longer accept invitations to go speak *about* people experiencing injustice. I had been invited to speak to a wealthy, all-white congregation located in the suburbs. The community the church was located in was predominantly Anglo, except for some small areas where immigrants lived. The immigrants worked at low-wage jobs, but they were mostly unseen, especially by members of the congregation I was speaking to.

Before I began my talk about the harsh reality so many immigrants face in the United States, the congregation immediately began to pepper me with questions not out of a sense of curiosity or wanting to identify with the reality so many undocumented immigrants face today, but rather, in an accusatory manner. Indeed, some of the questions I was asked were just plain mean. Questions like, "why are they stealing our jobs" (though, no one in that wealthy church could actually tell me of a time they had lost a job to an immigrant), "why do they bring crime and disease to our country," and "why don't they stay and build up their own country instead of coming here to drain our resources" were asked in one form or another. They weren't pleased by my answers so they kept asking me the same questions over and over.

When I was done I expressed some frustration with the leader at the total lack of compassion toward immigrants by people in the church. The leader responded defensively with, "well, we have compassion for immigrants who come the right way, but not for illegals." That was the day I quit what I call "poverty porn;" telling people stories designed to pull their heart strings but not harsh enough that they would actually feel compelled to do anything. I decided I would opt for helping people, especially those who are affluent, find creative ways to build relationships with people who are directly impacted by injustice.

Lesson: The Affluent Are Held Captive by Their Detachment from Those Experiencing Injustice

As we left off last chapter, after hearing the announcement of the impending genocide, Mordecai goes to the city gate and publicly mourns. He wants someone in particular to see his public witness of grief, his niece Esther.

What stands out at this point in the story is that Mordecai's attempt to get Esther to see him did not actually work. Esther did not look out of the palace and see Mordecai dressed in sackcloth and ashes at the city gate and then respond with appropriate action. Her handmaidens and eunuchs are the ones who saw him. In this instance, Esther was so secluded by her position in the king's palace and the affluence that came with it that she was not able to see even her closest relative in his moment of distress and the terror their people were facing.

Think about it. Even though the edict to eradicate the Jews emanated from the palace where she lived, it was not until she was alerted by her eunuchs and handmaidens to the fact that her uncle was by the city gate sitting in sackcloth and ashes, publicly grieving, that she responded. This means that the news of the edict that originated from the palace was not known to her until someone outside the palace communicated it to her. She was that detached from the suffering her people were experiencing.

Further, we know she was at least somewhat disassociated from what was happening to her people from her initial response to Mordecai. When she was made aware of her uncle's presence and condition at the city gate, "the queen was deeply distressed; she sent garments to clothe Mordecai, so that he could take off his sackcloth" (4:4). Esther, living in the lap of luxury where the highest of concerns, as we saw with the opening story of Vashti, is on outward appearances, responds in a way that she was conditioned to by her context: she sends down clothes. Her first concern is her uncle's appearance, not why he was fasting. Responding with clothes when someone is facing an impending genocide begs the question, "How can the church participate adequately in the suffering of the world if its participation is always at a distance?"[1]

Another question we must think about is, what would have happened if Mordecai accepted her gift of the clothes? If Mordecai accepts her well-intentioned though inappropriate gift, then his public protest is likely over. If his protest is over then Esther's conscience is relieved and Mordecai's worst fears will be realized. No matter how well-intentioned, there are times when acts of mercy done in response to an injustice that has been committed becomes an obstacle to achieving justice. There are moments when mercy can actually worsen injustice. This is just such a case.

Mercy and justice are typically not at odds with one another and we are not often forced to choose between the two. When vulnerable groups of people are impoverished or oppressed in some way, acts of mercy such as donating food and clothing can be helpful to meet immediate felt needs. People do need to be clothed and they need to eat!

Acts of mercy can also open the door for deeper relationships though this road must be travelled carefully. Sadly, church history is littered with churches steeped in affluence subjugating poorer churches simply because the more affluent church holds the checkbook. This kind of objectification of the poor and oppressed is colonialism, pure and simple, and serves primarily to relieve the conscience of the affluent church while leaving the unjust social, economic, and political orders intact, which, to no one's surprise, actually works to the benefit of the affluent.

Let me tell you a story. Years ago when I worked in an urban ministry I used to help set up short-term mission trips to our poor community for visiting affluent church groups. We tried to

---

1. Birch and Rasmussen, *Predicament of the Prosperous*, 93.

get these groups to take part in what we called poverty simulations—experiential learning weekends where they could learn
directly from the poor themselves and gain a greater understanding of what life is like for the urban poor. What we hoped is that
they would be so transformed they would want to return to their
homes and engage in learning relationships with the poor in their
own communities.

I remember one "Christian" high school who used to come
every year to our community to lead Vacation Bible Schools for
one of the low-income housing projects in our neighborhood. The
problem one particular summer was that by the time the principal
of the Christian high school called the dates for the Vacation Bible
School weeks had all been taken and the only dates open were for
the poverty simulation weekends. The principal began to try to
persuade me to move the dates around to better serve his group,
while I tried to reassure him that the simulations were actually
more transformative for the participants than leading the Vacation
Bible School programs. This was true. Though I ensured him his
students would be safe and would have a much more transformative experience, the principal continued to advocate for a VBS date
until, growing more and more irritated, he finally yelled at me,
"I'm not bringing my kids down there to learn from *those people*,
we're coming down there to *serve!*"

All too often our "service" to the poor removes any opportunity for incarnational relationships among the poor because we
share, in some way, the disdainful attitudes of this principal. The
poor are objects of our service, but not real people to learn from,
much less serve alongside of. Of course, this is not actually service
at all. This is not mercy at all. This is detached arrogance. This is
further objectification of the poor. This is colonialism. This is sin.
And it too often permeates much of what we call "missional outreach" in far too many affluent churches.

Mordecai does not want Esther's mercy. He doesn't need
clothes. Mordecai needs the edict which has been issued throughout the kingdom to be rescinded and that will require wholesale
policy change. It might even require some kind of leadership

change (which does happen to Haman in the end). He does not need her well-intentioned gifts. He needs her to advocate for justice. So he accepts nothing less.

To Esther's credit, his refusal was not met with hurt feelings. In this, Esther is contrasted with Haman, for both are in a sense rebuffed by Mordecai. But she seeks to learn; Haman sought only to destroy. Esther and Mordecai have a deeply personal relationship and so they have trust. Esther opts wisely to listen to Mordecai so she sends her servant Hathach down to her uncle to better learn what is really happening.

This shows us that when mercy is an obstacle to achieving justice, those most directly impacted by injustice should be allowed to decide what actions to take. For this to happen, it is necessary for those with access to resources to have incarnational relationships with those directly impacted by injustice so that those resources are not wasted, but put to the most effective and redemptive use. As we shall see, incarnational relationships are absolutely essential for genuine justice to be achieved.

Lesson: There Is a "Conspiracy of Detachment" That Maintains Distance between Those Directly Impacted by Injustice and Those Not Directly Impacted

Esther's initial response to the news of Mordecai's public mourning at the city gate reminds us of the tremendous gaps that exist between the reality that many poor and oppressed people face versus the interpretation of that reality from the vantage point of social, political, and economic privilege. This was evident in the opening story of the church wanting me to speak about immigrants but who were more interested in airing their baseless frustrations than in empathizing with the harsh life many immigrants are faced with. Oppression might seem merely like poor choices to some behind palace—or suburban—stained glass windows. These two widely different perspectives on the same context show that our geographical proximity, or lack thereof, to those experiencing injustice can have a tremendous impact on the way we perceive what the injustice is, whether it is injustice at all, and how we respond to the injustice.

The question we asked earlier still rings true, "How can the church participate adequately in the suffering of the world if its participation is always at a distance?"[2] I am convinced that the captivity to affluence that many are trapped in is partly due to our own choices and due partly to forces beyond our control. In essence, I believe that the distance between the affluent and powerful and the poor and oppressed is part of a "conspiracy of detachment." I want to look at three forces that make up this conspiracy of detachment:

1. our overreliance on individualism;

2. white flight from urban to suburban areas; and

3. the process of globalization that has shrunk the world into our local areas.

First, affluent detachment from those experiencing injustice is rampant when we are insistent on maintaining an over-reliance on individualism. Michael Emerson and Christian Smith studied evangelical Christians in the United States and their views toward racism. While the study is limited to those who identify themselves as evangelicals, I believe their findings hold great importance for everyone in the church in the United States as their conclusions illustrate that upholding an individualistic worldview creates detachment from those who are directly impacted by injustice. As a result, this not only prevents relationships with those who are marginalized by racism, but actually promotes the systems that perpetuate the causes of racism and related injustices.

Emerson and Smith hold that evangelicals profess their opposition to racism, but they tend to understand it solely on an individual level with very little recognition of the social, economic, or political reasons for its existence. If understood as a personal problem, then the answer to racism is going to be individualistic in nature rather than systemic.[3] They found that white evangelicals

2. Birch and Rasmussen, *Predicament of the Prosperous*, 93.

3. Emerson and Smith, *Divided by Faith*, 89.

having a variety of contacts, such as also having black acquaintances and living in a mixed neighborhood."[8] For whites to have a better understanding of the full impacts of racism is for whites to be immersed—incarnated—among numerous relational networks with African Americans. This occurs when these relationships help to form essential values and worldviews.

A lack of geographical proximity to the poor and the resulting absence of incarnational presence among the poor is the essence of detachment and continued captivity to affluence. Because our location significantly sways our understanding of Scripture and because Scripture has such a tremendous emphasis on the poor, the potential for affluent captivity and the resulting misuse of Scripture to justify affluent lifestyles is equally great. This is precisely why we have churches spending enormous sums of money on massive facilities while poor people struggle to adequately feed their children and pay for life-saving medications, sometimes occurring just blocks away from each other. It's nothing less than obscene.

The second aspect of the conspiracy of detachment has been through the flight of whites from urban to suburban areas. In his book, *White Flight*, Kevin Kruse looks at the city of Atlanta during the 1950s through the 1970s as the city experienced heightened tensions during the civil rights movement and the resistance of southern conservatives who hoped to maintain segregation. While Kruse's study is focused solely on Atlanta, I do believe there are similarities here that are apparent for all cities to look at. One of Kruse's main points in his book that counters current thought is that segregationists during that time did not simply give up, move out to the suburbs, and accept the new reality of racial equality. Something much more significant and transformative happened. Kruse states,

> Because of their confrontation with the civil rights movement, white southern conservatives were forced to abandon their traditional, populist, and often starkly racist demagoguery and instead craft a new conservatism

8. Ibid. Emerson and Smith's italics.

predicated on a language of rights, freedoms, and individualism. This modern conservatism proved to be both subtler and stronger than the politics that preceded it and helped southern conservatives dominate the Republican Party and, through it, national politics as well. White flight, in the end, was more than a physical relocation. It was political revolution.[9]

In the end, segregation was not just preserved, but began to be articulated as one of a long list of rights for whites while shedding the overt racism that was accompanied by the now-extinct Jim Crow laws. One could no longer call for the burning down of African Americans' homes, but one could defend segregated neighborhoods through defending one's rights to private property, making the assumption that the mere presence of African Americans would cause the devaluation of homes. Thus, they employed efforts to defend their neighborhoods from what southern white conservatives as well as white progressives viewed as deleterious influences.

This wasn't just a case of the Ku Klux Klan trading in their white sheets for business suits. The transformation included those who previously labeled themselves "progressive" on race relations. Kruse tells the story of Mozley Park, a neighborhood just west of downtown of Atlanta. When African Americans began to move into neighborhoods surrounding Mozley Park the resistance was led at first by right-wing racist groups like the KKK and others. But as the years passed something far more reputable sounding called the West End Cooperative Corporation (WECC) was formed. The WECC "helped establish an even more respectable homeowners' group, one that distanced the cause even further from the ugliness of its early days, while still ensuring the same result—the successful 'defense' of segregated neighborhoods."[10]

Kruse points out that the resistance to segregation was not just fought by individuals in certain neighborhoods; it was structural as well. This points to the forces at work to maintain the conspiracy

9. Kruse, *White Flight*, 6.
10. Ibid., 65.

of detachment. City planners and the Atlanta mayor's office set out to wall off black neighborhoods from white ones as much as they could. In the 1950s when highways were being built to link cities together, they were often built on land in black-majority neighborhoods. This was done in an effort to seal off white neighborhoods from black ones. This happened in cities across the country.

Even more, once African Americans began to move into white neighborhoods the assumption was that property values would begin to nosedive so that the neighborhood would become unlivable. Their fears were realized by their own actions as, "planners and zoning committees lowered their standards for the region and began approving projects they would have routinely rejected if the residents were still white."[11] This resulted in overcrowding as large apartment complexes were built, bars and other nefarious businesses moved in, and industrial warehouses began to spring up. The neighborhoods went through drastic changes and the responsibility for those changes, almost all negative, Kruse places at the feet of city officials. "The 'defense' of white neighborhoods was no longer the province of racial extremists seeking to sway the opinions of the working class, but instead something woven into the worldview of the upwardly mobile middle class, wholly respectable and admired."[12] Thus, geographical location greatly shaped the views of residents regardless of whether they were conservative or progressive in their political leanings. The subsequent detachment between whites and blacks was the product of white flight and adjoining actions by city officials which discouraged black neighborhoods from thriving and being a desirable place to live.

Finally, the last force that helps create the conspiracy of detachment between people directly impacted by injustice and those not directly impacted is globalization.[13] Cynthia Moe-Lobeda

11. Ibid., 74.

12. Ibid., 77.

13. One of the better resources that discusses the impact globalization has had on missional engagement is in Gregory Leffel's book, *Faith in Action*. He writes that the current state of globalization is, "at heart . . . the experience of

makes an important critique on globalization when she states that, "the prevailing model of economic globalization normalizes and dictates political-economic relationships that cripple human capacity to make decisions and take actions other than those that serve the utility of the market."[14] If we use Moe-Lobeda's critique in interpreting Esther's response to Mordecai, then we can say that Esther's initial response to Mordecai in giving him clothes certainly serves the utility of the power structure of the palace more than it does the cause of her people. While geographical proximity to those experiencing suffering and injustice is a crucial first step, we must go even further. We must identify with those who suffer, and see life from their perspective. This means we must be incarnated, or immersed in relational networks, among those who suffer. Incarnation crosses the barriers set up through detachment.

Esther's blindness to the reality Mordecai and the Jews scattered throughout the kingdom are facing and mourning at this time is not intentional on her part. Her captivity has been so subtle and unnoticeable and only becomes apparent when crisis arises and she is forced to respond to the unexpected news that her uncle is dressed in sackcloth and ashes and is mourning at the city gate for the world to see. She has momentarily lost her identity as she has become captive to the affluence of the dominant culture and society. Indeed, Mordecai later has to remind her that she too will suffer the same fate as her people if she fails to act.

---

the world as one place" (67). There are no longer places where globalization cannot be experienced in some way. The United Nations Centre for Human Settlements lists several ways that globalization has dramatically changed the way cross-cultural connections are made. They include (1) faster connections through increased and improved transportation and communication, (2) a greater number of options for connections are more available than ever before, and (3) the complexities of globalization means that connections between people from across the world are happening on multiple levels, including economic, political, cultural, technological, and social and they are happening oftentimes simultaneously. United Nations, *Cities in a Globalizing World*, xxx–xxxi. Globalization has certainly brought great benefits to communities, but it has also been destructive as well, particularly to poor and vulnerable communities.

14. Moe-Lobeda, *Healing*, 3.

However, before we judge Esther too harshly we should remember that she willingly risked her life to bring about justice. We would do well to recall that Esther's captivity is one that many in the church in the global North share today as residents in the most powerful and affluent nation in the history of the world. Moe-Lobeda illustrates this kind of captivity as she shows how mindless acquiescence to controlling ideologies and power structures like globalization can hang heavy on the daily activities of even the best-intentioned people living in the global North.

> It seems not strange, then, that people of relative economic privilege in the United States—though they may be compassionate and caring—agree to play soccer with balls made by child laborers; wear clothes made in sweatshops; eat strawberries grown on land that should grow beans and corn for its hungry children; buy stock in companies that dump toxic wastes in communities of color, devastate Philippine communities by deforesting their lands, and force subsistence farmers in India to buy seeds that will not reseed; and perpetuate an orgy of consumption that endangers Earth's capacity to sustain life.[15]

As we are able to redemptively utilize our access to the most basic of resources for the benefit of others, so too does our over-consumption of basic resources have potentially enormous damage for others as well. Connecting more with those who are harmed by even the smallest decisions we make can have long-lasting impact on our choices; from what we drive, to what we eat, to especially where we live.

Lesson: The Cure for Detachment and Affluent Captivity Is Incarnational Relationships among Those Directly Impacted by Injustice

A pervasive theme throughout Scripture is the truth that incarnational relationships among those experiencing injustice is the

---

15. Ibid., 68.

only way out of captivity to affluence and detachment. Esther had been immersed in her relationships with Mordecai and her Jewish people, which is why Mordecai needed only to remind her of her heritage. Jesus is able to be Savior to the world only because he came and immersed himself—the divine took on human flesh—so that he might know our struggles and fears as well as our dreams and hopes. To follow Jesus is to follow him into immersed relationships among people directly impacted by injustice.

One telltale sign of incarnational presence among the poor or oppressed is the existence of mutuality, where one side is not saddled entirely with giving or serving and the other is not weighted down with only receiving those services. Inherent in mutuality is that there is give and take between all sides in the relationship. Mutuality gives evidence that friendships are not one-sided; that this is not the case of the affluent having pity and taking paternalistic care of those who are impoverished and oppressed.

In 2003–2004, as part of my dissertation, I conducted a study of ten churches engaged in the ministry of resettling refugees. Five of the churches I observed and interviewed leaders at were engaged in political advocacy on behalf of refugees as part of their refugee resettlement ministries. Likewise, five churches did not engage in any kind of political advocacy on behalf of refugees. I wanted to find out what differentiated the churches that engaged in political advocacy on behalf of refugees from those that did not.

What I found out was that while all of the churches' ministries among refugees were vital and important, the primary difference between the group of churches doing political advocacy on refugee issues and those not doing that kind of political advocacy was entirely about incarnational relationships among the refugees they resettled. And incarnational relationships characterized by mutuality between refugee families and church members was decided largely by the proximity of the local church to where the refugees lived. For instance, when a church was located across a city, like Chicago or Minneapolis, from where the refugees were resettled, then the church lacked an incarnational presence among the refugees they resettled. When the church was located in the same neighborhood as where the refugees were resettled then there was an incarnational presence among the refugee families and mutuality likewise existed as well.

Mutuality between refugees and local church members took various forms. Refugees usually attended the church if they shared the same faith, often serving in leadership positions in the church. Refugees and church members developed deep friendships that went well beyond the time limits that churches had agreed upon to be responsible for resettlement, which varied but was approximately six months in length. Many of the church members I talked with who were engaging in political advocacy on behalf of refugees described the refugees as friends rather than as clients or people to whom help was directed. Thus, the political advocacy was engaged in, not so much because of where the members of the church stood politically or theologically, or whether the church members were rich or poor themselves. Rather, they engaged in political advocacy on refugee issues simply because they were close friends with the refugees themselves.

I remember one powerful story of a retired Home Economics high school teacher who was a member of a Protestant church that had helped resettle mostly Muslim refugees. The medium-sized city where the Muslim refugees lived had no place for the women to shop for clothes so the retired teacher gathered some sewing machines and the appropriate fabric and started a Thursday morning sewing club. Women from the refugee families came as did a number of women from the church and surrounding community. As they sewed together each week they also shared their stories together: their hopes, their dreams, their fears and their struggles. One thing that started emerging as the women shared with the others was that a number of the refugee women were either presently or had at one time been victims of domestic violence. As the refugee women shared this, a number of the women from the church and community also shared that they too had suffered similar experiences.

Sharing something so intimate made such a powerful impact on the retired teacher that she was crying as she told me this story.

This was the most powerful group she had ever been a part of. And this experience also greatly shaped what they advocated for politically. The retired teacher not only mobilized her church and community to advocate for more refugee funding in the federal budget, she also advocated strongly for such things as the passage of the Violence Against Women Act. She did all of this not because she liked or had a passion for political advocacy. In fact, she told me she hated everything having to do with politics. She mobilized and engaged politically solely because, as she tearfully told me, these issues impacted her friends. She was incarnated among her refugee friends and her advocacy emanated directly out of those relationships.

As in real estate, incarnational presence among the poor and oppressed is all about location, location, location. This is exactly what I found in my study. It was living in close proximity to the refugees more than merely knowing "about" the refugees that gave both impetus to advocacy and provided transformation of churches resettling refugees.

The level of engagement in the lives of the refugees increased dramatically when the church members welcomed them not only into this country, but even more, into their neighborhoods, their churches, and their lives. An intriguing finding from this study was that the members of the churches who resettled refugees, but yet who had not entered into incarnational relationships among the refugees and thus did not engage in political advocacy on refugee issues spoke themselves about the fact that they were not relationally close to the refugees they resettled. They admitted that the reason why they were not relationally close was because of the geographical distance that separated them—they lived in another part of the city and their isolation prevented incarnation. Yet, not one member of any of those churches ever mentioned the need to move the location of the church to be closer to the refugees they had spent so much time, money and energy resettling.[16] Instead, they opted to remain isolated. It is a good thing that Esther did not make this same decision.

16. Mefford, "To Set Free the Affluent," 223–24.

We see mutuality between Esther and Mordecai and the Jewish community when she agrees to approach the king with her request to stop the edict, which could very well end her life. In doing so, she requests that Mordecai "go, gather all the Jews to be found in Susa, and hold a fast on my behalf, and neither eat nor drink for three days, night or day. I and my maids will also fast as you do. After that I will go to the king, though it is against the law; and if I perish, I perish" (4:16–17). This is what incarnational relationships look like; I will use every resource I have to achieve justice for you because your struggles are my struggles, your dreams are my dreams, your fears are my fears.

The question before affluent and powerful local churches in the United States today is whether we will follow Esther's lead, remember our true identity in Christ (the one who intimately identifies himself with the poor and oppressed), and then be willing to risk our lives, our reputations—even our social standing—and utilize our access to resources to save the lives of our friends who are enduring suffering and oppression. Will we immerse ourselves in friendships with those who are suffering from injustice or will we remain captive to the affluence and status we benefit from?

If we are ready to engage in redemptive advocacy, then let's continue on. If you and your church are honestly lacking incarnational relationships among the poor and oppressed then put this book down, leave your church, your home, your neighborhood or whatever location you are trapped in and look for opportunities for even the possibility for incarnational relationships to occur. Then, after a year or two, pick this book back up and read chapter 5.

Lessons Recapped:

- The affluent are often so detached from those experiencing injustice that their affluence holds them captive, sometimes with devastating results as we see with Esther not being able to see or respond appropriately to Mordecai's public protest through mourning. There are times when mercy can inhibit justice from being achieved.

- There is a "conspiracy of detachment" that prohibits relationships between those directly impacted by injustice and those not directly impacted. The forces that make up this conspiracy include an over-reliance on individualism, white flight from urban to suburban areas, and globalization.

- The only cure for detachment and way of out of affluent captivity is incarnational relationships among those directly impacted by injustice. Incarnational relationships among those experiencing injustice are mutually transformative and liberational.

Questions for Discussion:

1. Do you think much of the church is held captive to affluence? Have you experienced this kind of captivity? How have you experienced liberation from this kind of captivity? Please share.

2. Can you name a time when engaging in mercy inhibited the greater need for justice of some kind?

3. If your team or congregation already can identify the injustice(s) present in your community, where are you in the process of becoming incarnated among those directly impacted by that injustice(s)? How have relationships among those directly impacted by injustice changed you or your congregation or community?

4. For those not engaged in political advocacy, would political advocacy be more accessible if the issue for which you were advocating impacted your closest friends? How does this impact the way we mobilize our congregations and denominations or religious networks for engagement in justice-related ministries?

Idea for Missional Engagement

This exercise is designed to help us see the prejudice in our own lives so it is good to center ourselves and remind ourselves to be honest as we take account of the relationships in our lives.

Take a sheet of paper and write down the names of the people I have listed below:

- Spouse or partner
- Children, grandchildren
- Parents, grandparents
- Siblings
- Cousins, aunts, uncles, other relatives
- Lifelong friends
- Work colleagues
- Neighbors
- People you attend church with
- Other organizations you are part of and the people you work with in those organizations
- People you know at the gym or through hobbies and activities
- People at restaurants or businesses you frequent and are familiar with
- People you most often interact with on social media

Now, beside each name, either write out "primary" beside their name or use a yellow highlighter to highlight which names function as "primary relationships." I am defining a primary relationship as one that is close and personal that has been sustained over time.

Once you identified all of the primary relationships now look at the list of the characterizations below. Draw a circle around the names that fit each characterization, including multiple circles if more than one characterization fits. If you do not know, then do not draw a circle.

- If they are a different race or ethnicity from you
- If they belong to a different socioeconomic class from you
- If they belong to a different religion from you
- If they have a different sexual orientation from you

Now, look at your list. Count the number of total names on your paper. Count the number of people who have circles. Is there a wide difference? Look at the names that are marked "primary relationships" versus the names that are not primary. Is there a balance in the number of circles between primary relationships and secondary relationships? Do you know of reasons for that? Are there things that you can to increase the diversity in your primary relationships? If comfortable with your team, this can be good to reflect on as a team and then to discuss how you can be more intentional in becoming more diverse in your closest relationships.

Action

5

A Step toward Unleashing

The Power of Shared Passion and Shared Vision

I remember a few years back meeting with some United Methodist leaders gathered together from around the state. These were the leaders of the conference's justice team, which met together several times throughout the year to lead the conference's work in justice-oriented ministries. I had been invited to come and listen to all that they were doing and offer some possible ideas for direction at the end.

What I heard both impressed me and troubled me. I was impressed by the number of events that were happening and the number of issues they were keeping track of. But I was also troubled by the fact that in talking about who was putting on or hosting the events, the same names of individuals and churches kept popping up. But even more, despite all of the activity, I could hear no overall purpose that was driving them or tying them altogether. Many of the events were ones that happened annually so they were regular responsibilities expected to occur regardless of what was happening in their state or the world. The questions that kept running through my mind were, "what are they building, what are they changing?"

I have seen this scene all too many times. The church has segregated justice work from the overall life of the church to a committee tasked to focus on a little of everything and who end up getting very little accomplished. Within the United Methodist Church, as with most denominations, there is a crippling dependency on and black evangelicals view racism very differently, though they often hold very similar theological beliefs. Black evangelicals generally see racism as impacting every aspect of society including schools, treatment by the police, the judicial system, voter enfranchisement, employment, and even churches. On the other hand, white evangelicals are generally unable to see the systemic impacts of racism or the benefits they accrue from living in a racist society.[4]

What is most pertinent here are the ways in which white evangelicals believe racism can be effectively addressed. White evangelicals contend that the United States will no longer be racist if everyone will simply "become a Christian, love your individual neighbors, establish a cross-race friendship, give individuals the right to pursue jobs and individual justice without discrimination by other individuals, and ask for forgiveness of individuals one has wronged."[5] What is noteworthy is how these suggested solutions are so steeped in individualism. By locating the solutions within an individualistic framework, any social, economic and political structures which perpetuate racism in society are left totally untouched and intact. Though white evangelicals condemn racism, allowing systemic racism to remain unaddressed through advocating only individualistic solutions means that they remain benefactors of the racist systems they believe they are condemning. "They do not advocate or support changes that might cause extensive discomfort or change their economic and cultural lives. In short, they maintain what is for them the noncostly status quo."[6]

Perhaps the most significant finding by Emerson and Smith for what we are looking at is that "having a close, cross-race friendship—or even two—has only minimal effects"[7] on the understanding of whites concerning the systemic nature of racism. Emerson and Smith find, importantly, that "changes in perspectives occur mainly in the context of interracial *networks* rather than merely having an intimate friendship. . . intimacy is less important than

4. Ibid., 91.
5. Ibid., 130.
6. Ibid., 130.
7. Ibid., 131.

THE FIG TREE REVOLUTION

structures to do the work of justice. An emphasis on efficiency has produced streamlined top-down vertical organizational models that look good on a corporate flow chart, but which discount the very heart of justice work: incarnational relationships among people directly impacted by injustice. As we discussed last chapter, incarnational relationships are what drive our engagement in advocacy and organizing. I do not want to entirely dismiss such committees. Indeed, all movements need internal organization. But the movement must drive the structural needs, not the structures trying desperately to drive the movement, which is what is happening in our dying denominations. When there is such a great emphasis on maintaining structural efficiency and the vision is one that is determined by the detached offices of the corporate hierarchy then the most important aspect of our engagement in justice is the easiest part to forget: relationships with people directly impacted by the issues that are worked on.

Lesson: What Are We Changing?

So, just before the meeting was about to end I asked them one question, a question I first learned from my friend and super-organizer Kristin Kumpf. This is a question I have now asked groups like this one dozens of times: "If we were to come back together exactly one year from today, what would be different as a result of your work? What would you have accomplished over the course of the next year that makes a difference in the lives of people directly impacted by injustice?"

As so often happens whenever I ask that question of teams, there was at first an awkward silence in the room. Then, as team members awaken they start to ask one another and even themselves, "what exactly have we been doing?" After a few minutes, another question usually begins to rise up, "where are we going and what do we want to change?" This is when we are ready to begin the work of setting a shared vision.

In the story of Esther the vision for change was obvious: repeal the edict that Haman coerced the king into signing which called for all Jews in the kingdom to be put to death. There are times when the need for change is obvious because the injustice taking place is so blatant and presents such a crisis. Still, even in those cases, Mordecai's passion to stop the genocide required that he act and communicate that vision with others. He began with Esther. As we discussed earlier, he communicated his vision beginning through his public witness of grieving at the city gate so that Esther could know what was happening. Mordecai showed that his vision was central to his mission because he did not want his refusal to obey other laws to distract from his central focus—repealing the edict that called for his peoples' mass murder.

Mordecai's passionate and single-focused pursuit of his vision ultimately reached the attention of Esther, the object of his public witness. Although we will focus more on building our teams to accomplish justice in the next chapter, a word on the need of sharing our vision is warranted. Mordecai recognizes that just sharing his passion to repeal the edict is not enough, he needs to appeal his vision to her self-interest. Remembering what we said earlier about self-interest, this term most often means discovering one's identity in deeper relationships among others.[1] Self-interest in the context of incarnational relationship is a powerful motivator for action.

Lesson: Knowing Where We Come from Helps Us Know Where We Are Going

A part of having a vision for where we are going and what we are changing is having a secure knowledge of where we have been. Mordecai reminds Esther of who she is and where she came from when they were communicating through Hathach about the need to repeal the king's edict. Mordecai told her, "Do not think that in the king's palace you will escape any more than all the other Jews. For if you keep silent at such a time as this, relief and deliverance will rise for the Jews from another quarter, but you and your

---

1. Bobo, Kendall, and Max, *Organizing for Social Change*, 111.

father's family will perish. Who knows? Perhaps you have come to royal dignity for such a time as this" (4:12–14).

Mordecai both appeals to her self-interest—her interests in the context of her people—by reminding her that she will not escape death simply because of her position, but rather, her position might actually be the thing that brings safety for all her people. Her fate is inextricably linked with theirs. His reminder to Esther of who she is and where she has come from was for the purpose of remaining single-focused on what lay ahead. Mordecai goes to Esther because she alone has the potential to redemptively utilize her position to secure the lives of her people. Thankfully, she shares Mordecai's vision.

However, as we discussed earlier, not every justice issue carries such obvious life and death implications. The work of organizing for social change cannot be done only when death is knocking on the door. Most times, unless we always have relatives who work in the same office as the decision-maker as Esther does with the king, waiting for the edict announcing the death of you and your loved ones will be a recipe for defeat. Thus, we must be looking ahead and building movements for justice long before the injustice comes. Sadly, this is often where local churches fail.

Lesson: Our Visions Must Be Proactive

I remember when states started passing anti-immigrant laws, beginning with SB 1070 in Arizona in 2010. Other states followed suit with similar draconian laws which gave law enforcement free reign to stop anyone for almost any reason, demanding to know if they had legal documents. Failure to have such documents resulted in long periods of detention and ultimately deportation. This was a terrifying time for immigrant communities in those states and many faith leaders responded quickly to the passing of such laws in their states. One United Methodist bishop took a strong stand against such a law that was in his state and he posted on the conference's website a powerful statement denouncing the law as contrary to the best intentions of faith.

What stood out to me however, was one of the comments in response to the Bishop's statement. It stood out to me because it was written by a member of the state legislature, which had just passed the law. The lawmaker said he was a United Methodist and this was the first time he had heard from his bishop that this bishop was against the law that he had helped to pass. Clearly, our prophetic statements once the act of injustice has been committed would not be necessary if we would be more proactive to stop it from occurring in the first place. It is far better to stop injustice than to sound prophetic after it has happened. As people of faith, we must be proactive. We must be visionary.

Without a vision we are always responding to the injustice and not setting a vision for what life should look like or how people should relate to one another. Setting a vision isn't about griping about what is wrong. Instead, we need to literally envision what we believe the world should look like ideally, and then utilize our resources to realize that dream in manageable steps. We fail at creating change because we do not take the time to set a vision for ourselves and because we spend our valuable resources reacting to the Hamans of the world as they set the agenda and then we rush around trying to defeat it. This is a recipe for defeat.

I have seen this all too often in the struggle to defend and support the rights of immigrants. Everyone who has watched their families and communities torn apart by raids and deportations knows that the struggle for immigrant rights is first and foremost a struggle for basic human and civil rights. The stories of immigrants are most commonly stories of people unable to protect themselves from human rights abuses in their countries of origin or victimized by globalized economies rigged to benefit the countries of the North and their affluent allies in developing nations. These are human stories of parents willing to risk their lives for the sake of feeding their families. These are also the stories of children who themselves are fleeing their countries, afraid for their lives, and seeking refuge.

As much as any other justice issue, undocumented immigrants are the Mordecais of today. Undocumented immigrants obey the laws of the land, they contribute to local communities, are leaders in their faith communities, and are raising their children to go even further in life and make even greater contributions. This is the typical life of the overwhelming number of immigrants. Further, our immigration system has emphasized the importance of family reunification and giving entry to immigrants from throughout the world rather than just Europe since 1965, when Congress made immigration a part of its emphasis on the pieces of civil rights legislation it was passing at the time.

Yet, in spite of all of this evidence, DC-based elite immigrants' rights advocacy organizations have repeatedly allowed this issue to be defined as an economic prosperity and national security issue rather than as a human rights issue. Before there is any opportunity to negotiate the details of legislation between those who favor reform and those who want to deport everyone and give defense contractors billions of dollars to militarize the southern border, the side for just and humane immigration reform has lost the argument because they have allowed the debate to be framed as an economic prosperity and national security issue. We instead must be visionary and define the framework of the issue from the way in which we envision the world to be: a place where all immigrants are valued and recognized for their contributions and work. Thus far, we have failed to do that.

Lesson: Our Vision Must Be Rooted in Relationships among Those Directly Impacted by Injustice

Our vision for specific and concrete change must be rooted in the Mordecais and Esthers of the issue—those directly impacted by injustice. Visions not rooted incarnationally but handed down by institutional leaders from on high, often lack the passion that must accompany visions for change. These kinds of "visions" should really be called directives and they are often one more example of colonialism that vulnerable populations must fight to control their own destiny and make their voice heard. It is a shame of the church that we too easily look for institutional direction rather than incarnational relationships that will guide us into the work of justice.

Visions of what we want to see changed or built over the course of the next year, two years, three years or longer are what guide all that we do. Our vision for concrete change keeps us free from the distractions that so easily sidetrack us. I know—easier said than done. Far too often in our churches our work for justice is drudgery, as seen in the story at the beginning of this chapter. It is endless and often purposeless committee meetings or hosting regularly scheduled calendar events that we pull off because it is that time of year again and not pulling it off seems more difficult to explain than actually doing it. Largely absent is the imaginative thinking about what we want to accomplish, how this will help build something larger, and how this will pull in people to share in the exciting work of creating change. We talk about our work for justice using words like *commitment* or *responsibility*—both important words!—yet we fail to emphasize the creativity and innovation that so often births real visions for change.

I remember, a while ago, having a conversation with a religious leader. I asked her about the vision for the work of the organization she led—where did she see the organization going in the next several years, what did they want to change, what did they want to build? Her response was startling in that she could not articulate any changes she wanted to make or anything concrete she wanted to accomplish. She and her organization could only repeat the institutional mandates that had been decided and handed down to them. Not surprisingly, that organization, over time, has indeed failed to build anything or change anything. There was no vision to do so in the first place.

When we talk about vision, Proverbs 29:18 comes to mind. It states, "Where there is no prophecy, people cast off restraint." Another translation uses the word "revelation" for prophecy, but both indicate that without guidance from God, there will be confusion, disorder, or even destruction. Indeed, the ungodly edict authored and planned by Haman for the mass murder of the Jews in the Persian Kingdom throws the city of Susa into confusion when it is read. Therefore, the opposite of this is order and progress toward the concrete change that is needed when there is revelation or prophecy, or vision as we have talked about.

Our visions for what we want to see changed in specific and concrete ways need to be shaped and formed by both the context in which we live and by revelation and guidance from Scripture. That is one of the reasons for this study in the first place. One of the mistakes local churches all too often make is that we opt for one or the other. We neglect the wisdom of the stories and teachings found throughout the pages of Scripture. Just as we have seen through the story of Esther and Mordecai, with appropriate understanding of the history and culture of the biblical passages we study, we can derive a tremendous amount of wisdom that can effectively guide us and empower us in our work for justice.

The other option we have a tendency to take is to hide ourselves away, cloistered in the study of Scripture and isolated from where people are experiencing suffering. One of the challenges for traditional seminary education is that far too much of it occurs in this kind of setting. While the skills for how to effectively interpret and exegete Scripture are necessary, the practical experience of living among people directly impacted by injustice should be much more prominently featured in any process of building leaders to serve the church and the world. To require only a handful of Sundays among the people of a local church out of a three to four year educational process that is supposed to equip leaders in our local churches is empty of real transformative education and certainly does nothing to train leaders in how to address contextual injustice.

Wayne Gordon began in the 1970s as a high school teacher while he and his wife led a Bible study for the youth of Lawndale, a neighborhood on the south side of Chicago. The community was poor and had some obvious problems that were typical of a lot of urban areas of that time. As the young group of believers began to form itself into a church they listed the challenges they wanted to address in their neighborhood. While they listed some of the obvious problems such as unemployment, drugs and crime, policing, health care, and education, when it came time to choose what they wanted to address first, Gordon was surprised by their choice: they wanted a safe place to do their laundry.[2] It was not what he would have started with, but by starting with something they could accomplish together—which they did—they were able to have confidence to build on that accomplishment and address more issues. Gordon had the sense to listen to his community and through their wisdom they began a long journey of transformation with a safe place to wash their clothes.

When there is more than one obstacle to overcome it requires listening to all of the voices impacted and coming to a consensus, if possible, of which issue they should rally around and try to accomplish. The question I asked of the group at the beginning of this chapter is necessary to shape our vision, especially in those contexts where there is more than one challenge that impacts peoples' lives. To state it again, if your group or team were to come back a year from now, what specifically would you want to see changed in your local context? What would be different?

I have seen all too often when groups come up with a "vision" that can never be accomplished, or at least you can never actually decipher whether a change has been made. Whenever I hear a team say their vision is to spread "awareness" about the epidemic of gun violence, or something similar, I ask them, "What will it look like when awareness has been spread?" The goal of raising of awareness is never a good goal to achieve. If Mordecai and Esther had decided they wanted to spread awareness of the edict announcing their impending genocide the genocide still would likely have proceeded. Their vision was to stop injustice, not just make people more aware of it.

2. Gordon, *Real Hope in Chicago*, 65–67.

Lesson: Our Vision for Change Must Be Specific and Concrete

Moving from a vague and ambiguous vision for change to a vision of achieving concrete and specific change is absolutely vital if change is to actually become a reality. Your local church and community group might want to make safer streets a reality for your neighborhood, but that is still quite vague. Breaking that down into smaller more achievable goals makes for a greater likelihood of success as well as bringing in more people to your work. So, working to make your community safer might begin with working with the city to build lampposts along the streets and in the parks over the course of the next year so that people can more freely walk at night. That is something that you will know you either accomplished or didn't accomplish.

The writers of the organizing manual for the Midwest Academy have a good set of criteria for establishing a vision that you can achieve and that can accomplish the most good. The list includes the following questions for your group to ask:

1. Will this change result in real improvement in peoples' lives?

2. Is this change winnable?

3. Will creating this change make people more aware of their own power to make change?

4. Will this change be evident to others and easy to understand by those not involved in the campaign?

5. Is there a clear decision-maker who we can focus our efforts on?

6. Is there a clear and workable time-frame that is achievable for our team?

7. Will our efforts create greater unity among those directly impacted?

8. Is this change in line with the morals and values of our team?

9. Will future leaders be built through our work to create change?[3]

If your team can answer these questions affirmatively, then you likely have a vision for change that has a high likelihood of success.

Struggles for justice are difficult and defeat is often more likely than success, but we will not even allow ourselves the possibility of success if we do not, within the context of a community of people directly impacted by injustice, dream of what life can be like absent the injustice that creates so much suffering.

Visions for creating change are not reserved only for clergy or people with titles or statuses either. Far too often, I have seen how those with statuses and titles can get in the way of real visions in the interest of preserving the status quo. Only those Mordecais and Esthers—those directly impacted by injustice and those incarnated among them—can genuinely dream of what change needs to happen in one, two, or three years from now. And how sweet it is when we work together to make that change a reality.

Lessons Recapped:

- Justice work must be directed by our vision for change. We must ask ourselves, "What are we changing? What are we building? If we came back together a year from today, what would we like to have seen changed by that time?"

- Knowing where we come from helps up know where our vision is taking us as our visions are rooted in our previous experience and relationships.

- Our visions must be proactive, anticipating the coming injustices before they happen because once an injustice happens we can too often only react while the other side sets the agenda.

- Our vision must be rooted in relationships among those directly impacted by injustice or else we will be guilty of

3. Bobo, Kendall, and Max, *Organizing for Social Change*, 23–26.

imposing change on groups that never had a voice. A vision for change is not a directive handed down from institutional leaders. Rather, it springs up from those most directly impacted by injustice.

- Our vision for change must be specific and concrete, or else how will we know we have achieved what we set out to achieve?

Questions for Discussion:

1. What issue(s) is your team most passionate about?
2. Why is there passion for these issues? Why is this important to you?
3. Do you know people directly impacted by this issue? Are there people directly impacted by the issue who are part of your team?
4. What are your collective answers to the questions for the Midwest Academy listed above?

Idea for Missional Engagement:

Continuing from the discussion questions above, if your team were to ask itself, "if we came back together exactly one year from today, what exactly would be different from where we are today?" what would be your answers? Once you have come up with an answer of something tangible that can be changed—a concrete change that benefits people directly impacted by injustice—have your team share why this is important to you.

Further, when looking at your vision for what your team is hoping to change and to build, is your vision proactive, anticipating the injustices that might likely occur to the people who are most directly impacted? Is your team constantly reacting to the injustices committed by the other side? If so, consider how you might think more proactively.

It is crucial as you begin or continue to have one-on-one conversations with others and invite them to be a part of the vision to make sure the vision is inclusive of others—especially of those directly impacted by the injustice you are addressing—and that it seeks to make concrete change among people directly impacted by injustice.

6

A Step toward Unleashing

When Two or More Are Gathered,
You Have a Team

When Rev. Emily Sutton arrived to begin her ministry in Columbia, South Carolina from Duke Seminary, she came at a unique time for immigrants living in the region. There was little being done in South Carolina by United Methodists in terms of organized outreach to Latino/as, and, as typical of many missional efforts, after selecting Rev. Sutton to lead the work, there was little done to genuinely support her in the enormous task she had before her.

She came to South Carolina in July of 2010, shortly after the state legislature followed the lead of Arizona in passing draconian anti-immigrant legislation. SB 20 forced everyone to carry identification papers at all times in order to demonstrate their lawful immigration status. Local police essentially replaced the function of the federal government's role in immigration enforcement, creating tremendous fear in immigrant communities throughout the state. It also gave free rein for the police to engage in racial profiling for it gave officers wide latitude—needing only "reasonable suspicion"—to stop people and ask for their papers. Needless to say, anti-immigrant sentiment in South Carolina, as in most of the United States at this time, was at a fever pitch.

Emily's ministry among immigrants in Columbia meant she was spending much of her time visiting people in jail. The people in her church, or their friends or loved ones, were constantly being picked up, often from simple traffic stops, and hauled off to jail. They were then handed over to Immigration and Customs Enforcement (ICE) officials where they were indefinitely detained and much of the time eventually deported. Seeing so many families torn apart was devastating to her efforts to build a viable local church. What's more, seminary had not prepared her for such a ministry context—no classes were offered on providing pastoral care for people forced to live in such dire fear of the local police.

So, sadly, she had to go outside the structures of the church to find the support and solidarity she needed. She connected with groups like Allianza Latina, which was working to build support networks for immigrants by getting community agencies to work together.

Rev. Sutton also realized the voice of the faith community could be a powerful one in South Carolina in defending and supporting the rights of immigrants and needed to be mobilized for that engagement. She realized that she could not improve the status of the immigrants in her ministry on her own efforts. She knew she had tremendous and untapped resources in her denominational ties that could be redemptively utilized for the benefit of others. Through one-on-one conversations she found other United Methodists in South Carolina like Sonya Brum who were natural allies. The United Methodist Conference had abandoned a task force previously set up so she began forming her own team through individual conversations with people that she suspected might share her passion. The conversations centered on recognizing the injustice that immigrants were facing and the need for the church to step up and do something to help.

The goal of her newly established team was to mobilize the United Methodist Conference in South Carolina to care for the needs of immigrants and to defend and support the rights of immigrants. To that end they wrote a resolution to be considered at the Annual Conference in the summer of 2011. They also tabled a sign-up sheet where they could have more conversations with interested individuals who might share their passion. The debate on the floor regarding the resolution they offered was intense, with one person in particular making despicable comments about immigrants and the need to deport them all. Rev. Sutton was so shocked by the man's comments that she stood up and gave an impassioned plea, reminding everyone that since she had planted a church among immigrants in Columbia, immigrants were no longer "those people" for United Methodists; immigrants, she reminded them, "are our brothers and sisters in Christ."

The resolution passed and Emily became known as the "pastor who gave the impassioned speech" which led to its passage. Her conversations with people at the table took on greater weight and meaning and she found more people who shared her passion. In one instance, another young pastor named Rev. Richard Reams approached her table to find out more information. Rev. Reams, who months before this might have shared some of the beliefs that immigrants just needed to "obey the law," was increasingly influenced by the plight of immigrants in the town where he served, Walhalla. His wife, Katie, was a social worker and saw firsthand the fear and confusion immigrants were living in. Richard shared Katie's shock at what immigrants had to endure just to live in South Carolina. At the table, he made a suggestion to Rev. Sutton about a more effective way to build her team and Emily smartly didn't just adopt the suggestion but recruited him to implement it. Viola! Another team member!

The South Carolina team went on to host numerous prayer vigils in support of immigrants, including outside the office of Senator Graham, an important swing vote on the Senate Judiciary Committee. They engaged in numerous efforts throughout the state to educate fellow United Methodists and South Carolinians in general about the contributions immigrants make to the state. They also met with members of the South Carolina legislative delegation to advocate for the rights of immigrants to be respected. Reverend Sutton and Rev. Reams even traveled to Washington, DC, to personally advocate their Senators and Representatives as to the importance of immigration reform.

To show the change that occurred among South Carolina United Methodists, at the 2015 Annual Conference, the conference devoted thirty minutes to highlight the work among immigrants and they received a passionate response from everyone there who seemed at last to recognize that immigrants were indeed their sisters and brothers in Christ. Change is possible! Even when it starts with one seminary graduate thrown into an impossible situation.

Lesson: Change Is Created through Teams, and Teams Are Entirely about Relationships

I share this story in detail to show how a team can be formed from scratch to overcome an impossible situation where the fear experienced among people directly impacted by injustice is so acute. I find many similarities between what happened among United Methodists in South Carolina and what happened in Esther's time. Though this story is named after one of the characters—and rightly so, considering her willingness to sacrifice her life for the safety of her people—we still see that injustice is most effectively thwarted, and righteousness is advanced, through groups of people passionately committed to the same vision. Though over-simplified versions of history like to water down historical events to individual heroes and their solitary stand against injustice, social change is almost always achieved through groups of people united by a common vision and shared passion. Change is created through teams.

Since it was Mordecai's refusal to pay homage to Haman which in many ways started this tragedy, Mordecai knew he had to recruit his niece who had a direct line to the king to advocate for his people to be spared. Mordecai and Esther both knew the danger she was exposing herself to by approaching the king, but both also knew she was the only one with this kind of access. Mordecai's decision to make a spectacle of himself at the city gate was for the greater good of alerting Esther to the impending doom. Mordecai had to realize two things at the time of his public witness: (1) he could not save his people on his own—he needed help;

and (2) he wasn't helpless—he had connections to the primary decision-maker.

This was similar to what Rev. Sutton realized in her own efforts for justice for her immigrant sisters and brothers. Both Mordecai and Emily knew they could not achieve justice through their own efforts and both took stock of their resources they had access to and used creative ways to mobilize those resources.

Mordecai rightly concludes that he cannot stop Haman's devious plan of destruction and so he plans to recruit Esther. As we saw earlier, at this point in the story Esther is held captive by her affluence and so Mordecai must work through her handmaidens and eunuchs, namely Hathach. Mordecai had taken action through his public protest through weeping in sackcloth and ashes at the city gate and Esther's initial response was less than enthusiastic to Mordecai. As a result, she sends Hathach, one of her servants, to talk with Mordecai one-on-one.

> Mordecai told him all that had happened to him, and the exact sum of money that Haman had promised to pay into the king's treasuries for the destruction of the Jews. Mordecai also gave him a copy of the written decree issued in Susa for their destruction, that he might show it to Esther, explain it to her, and charge her to go to the king to make supplication to him and entreat him for her people. (4:7–8)

Though this must have been a very emotional and distraught time for Mordecai, a man driven by his passion to protect his people from destruction, Mordecai seems from this description to be calm and thoroughly detailed in his approach to Hathach. He has already shown his passion and emotion through his public witness so he focuses on the details of the story so that Esther knows the full extent of the evil she and her people are facing. It is imperative that she act and emotion alone will not be enough to motivate her nor will it be all that she needs to know. Mordecai also knows that though Esther might be moved by his passionate public witness, Hathach might or might not be moved by this same passion. He is a servant in her court. So, Mordecai focuses on the facts more than mere emotion. He meets Hathach where he is.

Esther also recruits people to support her strategy as well. She told Mordecai,

> Go, gather all the Jews to be found in Susa, and hold a fast on my behalf, and neither eat nor drink for three days, night or day. I and my maids will also fast as you do. After that I will go to the king, though it is against the law; and if I perish, I perish. (4:16)

Though Esther was the one laying her life on the line, she so identified herself with her people at this point in the story that she wanted this effort to be shared by all those impacted and not just by herself alone.

It is the shared commitment to a single vision that makes teams powerful. Thus, it is vitally important, if you want to overcome injustice for you to link yourself with others in the community most impacted by the injustice at hand who share the same passion and vision.

The civil rights movement in the 1950s and 60s holds some of the greatest examples of teams being formed to overcome the most violent and virulent racism this or any country has ever seen. One of the movement's best organizers, Bob Moses, worked in probably the most violent state in the country at the time, Mississippi. James Silver called Mississippi the "closed society"[1] because the state was so controlled by its commitment to white supremacy. So violent was Mississippi that most organizations fighting against racism did not send any organizers there. That is, except for Bob Moses and the Student Nonviolent Coordinating Committee (SNCC).

Though organizers tend to be more effective the more they can personally identify with the struggles the people they are working with are feeling, Moses actually grew up in Brooklyn, far away from the small towns of Mississippi. Moses had graduated with a Master's degree in Philosophy from Harvard and was teaching

---

1. Taken from the title of James Silver's 1963 book about Mississippi, *Mississippi: The Closed Society.*

math classes in New York when the student sit-ins in February of 1960 captured his imagination and his passion.[2] Moses felt he had no choice but to go and join in the struggle he was witnessing from so far away.

It was through Ella Baker, a long-time leader in the civil rights movement and an advisor to the students leading the sit-ins, that he was connected with a man named Amzie Moore in Cleveland, Mississippi. It turns out that both saw the key for liberation for blacks in Mississippi was through political power. For Moses and Moore, desegregating public accommodations and school integration were important, but they both saw the key to black liberation was through gaining the right to vote. They spent a tremendous amount of time at the beginning—before they did any actions at all—just talking with one another. Moses listened intently to Moore describe the impacts of segregation on both blacks and whites in Mississippi. They traveled around the state as Moore introduced Moses to his contacts and the networks that were already in place.[3] This was the necessary time it took for Moore and Moses to share their vision and to become a unified team. This also illustrates for us that teams cannot be rushed into; relationships take time. Shared passion is something that always happens in one-on-one conversations.

For Moore, the attention and resources being poured into his state from groups like SNCC with people like Bob Moses, were welcomed as he had grown frustrated with the lack of leadership from the national offices of the NAACP. The best organizing is not directed from national offices, but is directed by those experiencing the injustice. Moore and Moses served as a vital team to boost activism in Mississippi as both needed each other and had a deep respect for one another. One colleague of Moses characterized their relationship as something akin to a father-son or student-teacher relationship. They needed one another, and

2. Dittmer, *Local People*, 102.
3. Payne, *Light of Freedom*, 105–6.

indeed, they had a unique relationship.[4] They shared the same passion and the same vision.

Lesson: The Heart of All Justice Work Is Relationships

The example of what Bob Moses did in Mississippi in partnership with local leaders like Amzie Moore shows us that the heart of organizing and advocacy—indeed, the heart of all justice work— is relationships. The soul of this book, the basis of everything I am writing is in these words: the heart of all justice work is relationships.

But how quickly we forget this.

I remember while I was in seminary I spent one summer working with youth in an inner-city mission in Cleveland. I was one of the few volunteers that had any prior experience in youth ministry and/or seminary education. Therefore, because I had some "expertise" I was asked to lead some of the Bible studies for the weekly camps that we were running for the youth. It took all of ten minutes in the very first Bible study I led for me to realize I had absolutely nothing to teach the urban youth of Cleveland. All of my "expertise" in youth ministry meant nothing in a context that I knew little to nothing about. Realizing this, I quickly changed the structure of the study and for the rest of the summer I learned from the kids who went through the summer camps as we discussed what it took to live as a Christian youth on the streets of East Cleveland. No seminary class could have taught me more than I learned that summer. I was transformed. The youth learned to contextualize Scriptures to their local situations as those of us who led the studies refused to teach; we just asked questions. Reading and studying Scripture must be done in the context where there is real suffering, and needs to be led by those experiencing the actual suffering.

4. Ibid., 63.

It is vital that if we are not rooted inside a community experiencing forms of injustice that we approach the people in that community as Bob Moses and Esther did; we must learn first. Esther sent Hathach to learn from Mordecai what was happening. Mordecai gave Hathach a copy of the exact edict read to the city of Susa so that Esther would know the enormous power she was facing.

Mordecai had shown his emotions with his public witness and then he focused on the details Hathach needed to share with Esther. Thus, a team needs to be formed around both of these elements: the passionate emotion that comes from staring injustice in the face and the factual information of what has happened and what needs to happen to bring about justice.

Teams are more than committees because the members of the team share the same passion and the same vision for concrete change. Teams are not email lists or regular committee meetings that get together because, you know, "we always meet on the first Tuesday of the month!" Local churches need more teams and fewer committees. Teams are groups of people with shared vision and shared passion.

And it is crucial to share the same passion. When I first started working with United Methodists across the United States I quickly learned that some of the established conference committees were made up of people who each had their individual passions for specific issues, or even worse, committees sometimes consisted of some people who had little passion for justice at all! Thus, it was oftentimes impossible to corral those passions into meaningful and effective direction. This is one of many problems with attempting to achieve justice through institutional structures.

Instead, we need to look to the relationships like Mordecai and Esther, or Bob Moses and Amzie Moore. These were relationships formed over time, rooted in geographical proximity, and shared experiences. Appointing people from various regions of a state (or sometimes multiple states) to sit in a room every few months or so and design an effective strategy for mobilizing a conference into justice-related ministries is not going to be effective.

This is not a team and as we have seen, teams of people with shared passion and shared vision create change, not committees.

Lesson: Personal Ties Are Stronger than Ideological or Institutional Commitments in Our Work for Justice

Our organizing and advocacy is meant to be entirely based in relationships; relationships with those directly impacted by injustice, relationships with other allies working toward the same vision for change, and relationships with the decision-makers to whom we advocate. As we seek to redemptively use our access to resources to gain such access for those whose access has been denied—which we refer to as redemptive advocacy—we can only be as effective as we are based in incarnational relationships among those directly impacted by injustice.

National church hierarchies throughout history have proven incapable of effectively mobilizing their own denominations for the work of organizing and advocacy. In the research for this study and in my other readings in fact, I have yet to find historical evidence of any mainline denomination whose own internal structures or agencies have effectively mobilized and organized the members of that denomination to engage in large scale political advocacy. Denominational members are most certainly involved in these movements for justice, but it is through outside organizations more concerned and focused on building grassroots teams that this is accomplished. Helene Slessarev-Jamir contends that denominational involvement in justice movements has been coordinated primarily by outside organizations because denominations have different priorities from those of local churches.[5] Surely much of the difference in priorities is due to the fact that local churches are most often rooted in the communities where the injustice is occurring and national hierarchies are focused on issues of institutional maintenance.

5. Slessarev-Jamir, *Prophetic Activism*, 6.

Thus, the most effective teams are local expressions of local concerns and passions. Teams are inherently relational and will not grow because someone from on high has mandated that a committee meet. Instead, teams are created out of shared passion and shared vision, and the heart of this is always rooted in a local context. Teams are built through one-on-one conversations, just as they were between Bob Moses and Amzie Moore. As a result, Moore opened the doors to the networks he was part of and allowed Moses to meet with other leaders throughout the state. This is how the movement was built in Mississippi and this is how any movement is built whenever and wherever there is a struggle to overcome injustice.

In another study about Mississippi and the civil rights movement we see not only how teams made up of people with shared vision and shared passion changed the highly racialized context of Mississippi, we also see how these teams transformed the team members as well.

Doug McAdam studied the 1964 Freedom Summer when mostly northern white liberal college students traveled down to Mississippi to assist SNCC in registering blacks to vote. In this study, McAdam in part explores the differences between students who signed up to go to Mississippi and did not go—those he calls the no-shows—and those who did participate in Freedom Summer. Most important from this study was the fact that when students signed up to go as members of a group or network from their home campuses, they were much more likely to follow through and go to Mississippi than the students who signed up individually.[6] The no-show students held the same ideological commitments as the students who did go to Mississippi, at least prior to the time of leaving for Mississippi. But the reason for not showing up, McAdam surmised, was because the no-shows had no "personal ties" to the project.[7] Personal ties were stronger than ideological or institutional commitments.

6. McAdam, *Freedom Summer*, 65.

7. Ibid., 64.

This is why it is so crucial for us to view teams as more than mere committees. Teams, instead, are organisms—a complex whole of interdependent parts working together to achieve some specific end. Teams are innately missional in that we are part of a set of relationships designed to accomplish something, to create change, to stop the suffering being unfairly inflicted on some specific group of people with whom we are intricately connected.

Mordecai recruited Esther, who then recruited Mordecai and all of the Jews in Susa and in the end they saved the lives of the Jews living under the threat of genocide. Bob Moses was recruited by the bravery of the students at North Carolina A&T in February 1960, and then, under the direction of Ella Baker, connected with Amzie Moore, who then recruited other SNCC students who recruited other grassroots leaders throughout Mississippi and elsewhere in the South that brought about the 1965 Voting Rights Act. Jesus recruited his twelve disciples who after his death, and the suicide of his one betrayer, in turn recruited the people of Jerusalem, Samaria and beyond who ultimately changed the course of human history.

Teams that share the same vision and the same passion are the only way that injustice is ever overcome.

Lesson: Teams Are Made Up of People Who Were Invited to Participate

Lastly, creating a team of shared vision and passion is an intentional act. People must be asked. In my dissertation research which I discussed earlier, I interviewed fifty-five people from local churches involved in refugee resettlement ministries and the first question I asked each of them was how they got involved in this kind of ministry. Every single one of them had the same answer— they were asked individually. No one talked about fancy bulletin inserts or a dramatic appeal from the pulpit or about institutional or hierarchical mandates. It was all about having a one-on-one conversation with someone who shared the vision of resettling refugees, and their passion for doing so, and then asking them to be a part. Each of them said yes. They weren't being asked to join a committee, they were asked to join a ministry, an activity, a team. Connecting with people who have similar passions for people directly impacted by injustice is the essence of team-building. Teams are the only thing that has ever changed the world and teams are the only thing that will ever bring about change in the future.

Lessons Recapped:

- Throughout history, any time systemic change happens, that change is always created through teams, or groups of people with a shared vision and a shared passion.
- The heart of all justice work is relationships.
- Personal ties are stronger than ideological or institutional commitments in our work for justice because, again, the heart of all justice work is relationships and teams are about relationships; a group of people with shared passion and shared vision.
- Teams are made up of people who were invited to participate because teams are not about institutional mandates or fancy pleas from the pulpit; teams are about relationships.

Questions for Discussion:

1. Name a time when you were invited to participate in a project or the planning of an event or campaign of some kind by someone else. Would you have participated had you not been invited personally?

2. Considering the injustice(s) that exists in your community, have you heard the passions that others in your church or team share about why they are working for justice? If so, what resonated in you when you heard them share their passion?

3. Name a time when you felt in over your head in some kind of missional work. How did you learn how to cope? Who did

you lean on? If you are one who is not directly impacted by injustice, how can you approach those directly impacted as learners?

4. Is your team rooted in relationships with those directly impacted by injustice? Are they reading this book with you? Are there ways for their voices to be heard first and foremost? How are decisions made and can the voices of those directly impacted by injustice figure more importantly in deciding the direction you move in?

Idea for Missional Engagement:

If you already have a team, no matter how small, practice sharing your vision and passion with one another. It is good to hear from one another and it helps when we share our own reasons why we are passionate about creating change. Break up into groups of two and have one share why they are engaged in this work and then have the other person do it.

Also with your team, have each member write down three people you believe might be interested in sharing your passion and then covenant with one another to make time to invite them to be a part of your team by having a one-on-one conversation where you share your passion and vision for the change you hope to create. Do this in one week's time. Why one week? Because we are tempted to conveniently forget if we wait any longer. Make sure when you have your one-on-one conversation with them that you invite them to think of others that they can invite and then follow up with them when they begin having one-on-one conversations and making invitations to others.

7

A Step toward Unleashing

Strategies for Making the Vision Real

I n January of 2015 Senator Grassley (R-IA), who chaired the
Senate Judiciary Committee, stood on the Senate floor and de-
clared he would not support any legislation that would lessen the
sentences for low-level, nonviolent drug offenders. Since he was
chair of the committee and essentially decided the agenda for what
bills the committee would look at, his statement meant that any efforts to enact sentencing reform legislation were seemingly futile.
Although the prison population has ballooned in large part due to
long and racially biased sentences for low-level drug offenses, the
hope for reducing the number of people incarcerated seemed to be
all but lost for criminal justice reform advocates.

Hope may have been lost for many advocates, but it wasn't for
the people of faith in Iowa.

People of faith in Iowa had long been concerned about the
criminal justice system, both at the state and federal level. The
main stumbling block to Grassley being better on this issue was
his staffers. What we needed was for Senator Grassley to hear
directly from his constituents. The good thing for us is that Senator Grassley, to his credit, tends to be very receptive to messages
from Iowans about what they care about. But we had to get their
voices directly to Senator Grassley's ears and not through the
filter of his staff.

The truth was that many faith leaders in Iowa either had personal experience with the criminal justice system themselves or

through their families or loved ones. Many faith leaders pastored churches where their parishioners were impacted as well. One powerful church, Women at the Well United Methodist Church, is actually located in a women's prison in Mitchellville, Iowa. They are a living witness of God's grace as they experience firsthand the brokenness of the criminal justice system as well as the grace and joy of the Body of Christ.

So, in partnership with the DC-based faith coalition working on criminal justice reform Iowa clergy wrote a letter to Senator Grassley urging him to allow sentencing reform legislation to pass through his committee. They did not insist that he author the legislation; just let it proceed. That was followed by an editorial in the Des Moines Register signed by three Iowa bishops, urging the same thing, which was then followed by an editorial also in the Des Moines Register urging Senator Grassley to follow the advice of the clergy in his state.

There was even more activity, including opportunities for all Iowans to call and use social media to urge Senator Grassley to allow the legislation to proceed and a unique conference call between Senator Grassley himself and some of the Iowa clergy leaders. The Iowa clergy on the call, led by Rev. Abraham Funchess and Rev. Lee Schott who pastors the Women at the Well United Methodist Church, spoke with authority about how sentencing reform legislation would impact their congregations and benefit the country as a whole.

And it worked. Though Senator Grassley began 2015 dead-set against sentencing reform legislation, by May he gathered together six other Senate offices to work together on a bipartisan sentencing reform bill. By October of that same year, the Sentencing Reform and Corrections Act, spearheaded by Senator Grassley, had passed out of the Senate Judiciary Committee, 15-5.[1] In the more than ten years I worked on ending mass incarceration, the incredible work by the Iowa clergy provided an excellent example of how the faith

---

1. As of this writing, the legislation was not passed, but we are ever hopeful for this to pass in a new Congress!

community can literally move mountains in order to bring about change for those directly impacted by injustice.

Lesson: Vision and Passion Need Strategies to Succeed

One of the things this opening story shows is that even with a shared vision and the one-on-one conversations to recruit people into their team, teams need strategies to bring about change.

In the story of Esther we see Mordecai's strategy first through the location of his public grieving. He wants Esther to see his public witness. He doesn't assume that just because she lives in the palace from which the edict emanates that she will know about the possible holocaust and will then take action. There is a sense that Mordecai suspects that Esther is captive to her affluence and position of power as he stays outside until someone is sent to speak with him. Mordecai leaves nothing to chance.

Mordecai knew Esther was in a unique position and that this was the most ideal time for her access to the king to be utilized redemptively ("for such a time as this"). While Mordecai can be given credit for awakening Esther to the seriousness of the situation, the strategy for approaching the king to ask for a reprieve has to be credited to Esther. Esther asks for the spiritual support she knows only her community can provide by asking Mordecai to mobilize every single Jew in Susa to fast and pray for her for three days. Esther knows she has access to few resources so she wants to use every resource within her grasp as she risks her life.

Esther ultimately decides to approach the king where she will dramatically plea for the safety of her people and point out the devious manipulations of Haman. Esther knew that initiating an approach to the king could easily not end well. I am sure Esther must have felt a tremendous amount of fear as she waited to see if the king would hold out his golden scepter signaling his acceptance.

I cannot help wondering, as she awaited her fate, if her thoughts drifted to Queen Vashti. As we discussed at the beginning of this study, Queen Vashti is the former queen who refused to obey the king when he called for her while he was eating and drinking with his friends. King Ahasuerus is so offended by her refusal to come to him that upon consulting with his advisors he banished her from the palace and his presence forever. But Esther had done all she could to make her advocacy to the king a success and that is what strategies are all about.

Lesson: What Strategies Are and How They Can Be Used to Realize Our Vision

Employing successful strategies entails knowing what a strategy is in the first place. The Midwest Academy is helpful in clarifying the difference between having a plan and having a strategy.

> If your objective is anything other than making an official do something . . . then you don't need a strategy, you only need a plan. The difference is that a plan is about the steps you will need to take for any project, while a strategy involves the relationship of power between you and the [decision-maker].[2]

One danger in the use of strategies is that too often strategies can replace the vision itself as we end up focused on attaining a certain number of prayer vigils rather than winning a vote on a piece of legislation or flipping the position of an elected member of Congress. Just as Esther decided to have her people pray and fast for three days as well as her servants, strategies are meant to mobilize our resources to alter the position of the decision-maker so that they would take the action we are advocating for.

The opening example to this chapter illustrates the various strategies that were used toward the overall strategy of changing Senator Grassley's (the decision-maker's) views on sentencing reform. Some of the strategies we used included:

- pressure from both the grassroots (clergy letter and a couple of call-in days) and grasstops (Bishops op-ed);

---

2. Bobo, et al., *Organizing for Social Change*, 30.

- media exposure (*Des Moines Register* editorial and a Twitter thunderclap); and

- direct advocacy (fly-ins of clergy, in-district meetings with staff, and a conference call between Senator Grassley and Iowa clergy).

The end result was that the people of faith in Iowa did the unthinkable, they flipped Senator Grassley's position on sentencing reform and he became a principle architect in sentencing reform legislation.

Lesson: Entrenched Power Is Far More Fragile than It Appears

One of the lessons of this story that helps determine how we develop our strategies is the fragility of entrenched power. To do as the king did to Vashti—to banish someone for life for refusing to come into your presence and then legislate patriarchy, which was already societally practiced—shows how fragile he and his advisors considered the patriarchy to be. In addition, for Haman to resort to such an abuse of power—to murder an entire race of people because he was offended by one man—reveals that his sense of power could be destabilized by even the slightest defiance. Though Haman and the king have all the power of an expansive kingdom at their fingertips, they are easily sensitive to even the smallest of challenges.

Access to all the power in the world, literally speaking in these cases, does not create a sense of security for those who hold the reigns. Institutions and hierarchies are oppressive to vulnerable people when the power associated with the institutions and hierarchies is used for the benefit of the few elites in control rather than for the benefit of the common good. Yet, our hope lies in the truth that even the most oppressive of institutions and hierarchies can be toppled through the most unsuspecting of sources.

I remember seeing how fragile entrenched power was in 2006. It was that year when the effort to pass what was known then as "comprehensive immigration reform" was in dire trouble as the

House had passed draconian legislation that would have not only made undocumented status an aggravated felony, but also would have made offering aid to undocumented immigrants a criminal act. The fact that the Senate legislation was not all that much better made things look and feel pretty bleak. Indeed, anti-immigrant forces in Congress seemed intimidating.

I felt a little intimidated myself until I joined my colleagues from a number of faith offices who were invited to a meeting with Representative Tom Tancredo (R-CO). Tancredo, at that time, was the leading voice in Congress calling for the deportation of all undocumented immigrants in the United States. Rep. Tancredo was also known for being a committed evangelical Christian and he wanted to meet with us to see if we could come to any kind of common understanding about our theological differences.

Though we disagreed, it was a polite meeting. About ten minutes into the meeting one of my colleagues asked him to give his biblical basis for why he believed all undocumented immigrants should be deported and the border should be sealed. He thought for a few seconds and then said, "We have to realize that this is a struggle between two civilizations . . . no, this is a struggle *for* civilization." Mr. Tancredo was a nice man, but the biblical basis for his stance was entirely specious and untenable. It didn't exist.

We of course ended the meeting having found no common ground, but I left knowing that though it would take a long time (little did I realize how long), the moral struggle for immigration reform would ultimately win because the forces working to deport our undocumented sisters and brothers had absolutely no moral or theological legs to stand on. Though anti-immigrant forces have enormous resources behind them, though they regularly lie about the impact that immigrants have on local communities and the nation as a whole, and though those lies have found willing accomplices in much of the U.S. media and so-called political leaders (including now the president), I left feeling emboldened that we were right and that the moral basis of the anti-immigrant side was faulty and cannot long stand.

This is important in the strategies we employ because we need to find the weaknesses of the side fighting against us and then counter them with our strengths. Ever since the meeting with Rep. Tancredo, the messages we used as a faith coalition were much bolder because we knew that the other side had no plausible theological basis. For Esther, once she was able to get the attention of the king and present herself in his good graces she could shine the light on the manipulation that Haman had used to coerce the king into signing the edict. Finding out the weaknesses of who or what is fighting against us will help set in place necessary strategies that will expose their weaknesses and highlight our strengths.

Lesson: Working for Justice Will Inherently Involve Conflict

Any effort to create change will inherently involve conflict. When entrenched power is creating harm for ourselves and the people we love, conflict is unavoidable. This is often challenging for faith communities as so many in the church tend to shy away from conflict. We want change, but we hate conflict and since change inherently involves a conflict between what is and what should be, we too often opt for the status quo since it is what we know and what we are comfortable with no matter how unjust that status quo might be. However, being an agent of change means that we must become intimately aware of and engaged in peaceful mediation when there is conflict. And when there is the presence of injustice that is being covered up by the premise of false peace, we might even have to create the conflict that will lead to genuine shalom; the presence of justice for all people without which there can never be peace.

I remember several years ago being part of a group of faith leaders who met with the notorious Sheriff Joe Arpaio, the Arizona sheriff who has been investigated by the Department of Justice for denying immigrants in his jail their basic human rights and for openly engaging in racial profiling. He is the poster boy for harsh and punitive immigration enforcement policies. I sat at the table with several faith leaders who bent over backwards to avoid any confrontation with Sheriff Joe, one even asking what advice he had for people of faith! This was our one opportunity to speak out for those who had been and continued to be so poorly treated by this racist sheriff, and the "faith leaders" chose their own safety and comfort instead of confronting him with the harsh and uncomfortable truth of his actions and then inviting him to treat immigrants more humanely. It was, in essence, an invitation to his own liberation that was never offered because the leaders chose capitulation.

This is a crucial point to make. When confronting decision-makers, particularly ones who are not known for their benevolence, we need to be honest and bold while yet invitational. Honesty and boldness means we name the injustices that have been done, while granting the invitation to liberation to those responsible for the injustice. This does not mean, however, being rude. I have seen people in meetings with decision-makers supposedly "speak truth to power" and use this as a thinly veiled excuse to be jerks to someone they simply do not like. This is just selfishness because we are ruining the opportunity for those directly impacted by injustice to have a chance at justice for the personal pleasure of publicly embarrassing the decision-maker. That helps no one and usually cuts off communication entirely.

But it is equally selfish to avoid honesty and boldness altogether like the faith leaders did with Sheriff Arpaio. In so doing, we might make ourselves look good with the person in power, but the decision-maker is never given the opportunity to be held accountable for the injustice that is happening and their responsibility to provide needed relief. Jesus calls all of his followers to engage in the holy act of redemptive advocacy. We do this because this has been done for us. This is the ultimate act of love and it must be done in honesty, boldness and with genuine invitation. Because advocating for justice inherently involves conflict and because churches are so often conflict-avoidant, we must be mindful to sensitize people to the need to be comfortable with conflict.

Lesson: People Will Likely Engage in Organizing and Advocacy when They Understand It Is Consistent with Their Existing Values

Another reason many people have apprehension about engaging in organizing and advocacy is because they do not see this work as consistent with their existing values and experiences. In short, political engagement does not feel Christian or "churchy." However, when we base our engagement in advocacy and organizing on incarnational relationships among those directly impacted by injustice, then we are able to show the people whom we hope to recruit into this work that it is indeed missional. Advocacy and organizing is essentially biblical and missional as these actions are a vital way for people to express their love and compassion for the people directly impacted by injustice.

The first year I began mobilizing United Methodists to host in-district meetings with their members of Congress to urge their support for immigration reform, I was able to get about six meetings set up. That hardly was enough to have any national impact. A year later, I didn't call them "in-district meetings with members of Congress," but instead, called them "Neighbor to Neighbor" meetings. We went from six the year before to fifty. Neighbor to Neighbor meetings also came with a toolkit that explained every step of how to set them up, implement them, and then do the necessary follow-up. People need to know how to do advocacy and organizing as much as they need a biblical and missional framework for it. With the Neighbor to Neighbor meetings I made sure the action was compatible within a missional framework: local churches acting as mediators between their members of Congress and their newly arrived immigrant sisters and brothers. This was the reason why there was a dramatic rise in numbers and the greater impact on the overall debate.

Using a missiological framework will lead to greater engagement in advocacy and organizing among those directly impacted by injustice and those incarnated among those directly impacted. Once your team becomes involved in the missional work of advocacy and organizing your team members will most likely become more sophisticated in their understanding of effective advocacy and the need for more daring and effective strategies. I saw this process at work firsthand.

Under the Obama administration there had been widespread deportations of undocumented immigrants. In 2010 I called a number of our United Methodist grassroots leaders to test their interest in participating in civil disobedience actions to put an end to the deportations and there was little interest. While there was no questioning their commitment to defend and support the rights of immigrants, this step was just beyond the comfort level of where they and their teams were at that time.

However, by 2014, after deportations persisted and after United Methodist leaders had engaged in numerous public witness events and had several years of organizing and teambuilding under their belts, I again asked our leaders if there was any interest in engaging in civil disobedience as a strategy toward ending deportations. The answer was overwhelmingly yes. We ended up leading two different direct actions of civil disobedience: once on President's Day in February that I mentioned earlier and one later in July of that same year.

For the one in July we had no funding to fly in any of the participants so I just put out the call for folks to come on their own. Though I probably shouldn't have been, I was shocked at the response. In a matter of just weeks, fifty United Methodists participated in the action including two van loads of people driving all the way from Iowa (who stayed in my home—I love Iowa!). Everyone came on their own dime. You know why? Because they were either immigrants themselves or they were incarnated among immigrants and they understood that we needed to do everything—including getting arrested in front of the White House in an act of civil disobedience—to stop the fear.

It wasn't long after the July action that President Obama expanded his earlier Executive Order, providing temporary legal status for certain groups of undocumented immigrants. Change does happen when we employ strategies that take us to the consciousness of our vision and when we step out boldly in love.

Lesson: We Need to Honestly Assess Our Resources to Mount Successful Campaigns while Employing Every Ounce of Creativity We Have

One lesson from Esther and Mordecai I want to emphasize is the importance of creativity in our efforts to create change. When sizing up the forces aligned in opposition to the change we envision creating, it can be tempting to feel intimidated and to belittle our own resources in comparison. It also is tempting to base our ability to create change on our financial resources alone and to forget the limitless creativity we have at our disposal.

For Esther, her greatest resource was the unique love God had consistently maintained throughout history for the people of Israel and she intended to utilize that for the good of her people. So, she instructs Mordecai to have every Jew in Susa fast and pray for three days, a brilliantly strategic move, heightening the expectations and dependence for herself and her fellow Jews on the power of God.

We will do well to follow Esther's lead in taking stock of our resources in our struggles for justice. I have seen numerous creative liturgies used in worship services that collectively express concern for the injustice that is present and the belief that love and justice will ultimately overcome. One of the powerful ways worship can be effectively utilized in the struggle for justice for the most vulnerable is to create a picture of the world for people—both for those directly impacted by injustice as well as those directly culpable—that we envision without the presence of injustice. Even more than sermons, things like:

- songs,
- Scripture readings,
- testimonies from those directly impacted,
- bulletin inserts with stories of those directly impacted,

- short videos for worship or Sunday school classes, or
- corporate prayers by the entire congregation.

All of these are powerful ways to raise awareness and to introduce the congregation to the need for advocacy and to invite people to collectively engage in worshipfully envisioning the world God desires us to live in; a world that can be realized through advocating and organizing for justice.

You will notice I did not include sermons in the list above. This is because listeners can easily remain passive and disengaged during a sermon. Further, the last thing you want is a bad sermon on the issue you are advocating for as it tends to turn off potential team members. Stories about those directly impacted by injustice that are inserted into sermons on other faith-related issues are much more effective in engaging listeners and are much more likely to be remembered.

Another strategic and sometimes overlooked resource in the faith community is networks—both institutional and organic (though the more effective ones are almost always organic). Networks are sometimes our greatest resources when we come face to face with seemingly immoveable forces of injustice.

I remember when President Obama came into office with promises to bring immigration reform legislation before Congress in his first two years in office. We had high hopes as advocates for reform that were soon dashed as he began to detain and deport hundreds of thousands of immigrants each year. His administration claimed that they were just deporting "criminal aliens" but we knew better. A number of us who worked in faith offices in Washington DC had met repeatedly with staff from the White House and the Department of Homeland Security (DHS) to urge them to stop these inhumane raids that were tearing apart families and entire communities. But we were getting nowhere. The meetings were becoming dull and repetitive and White House and DHS staff were becoming immune to our messages.

In 2010 we were set to have yet another meeting with the same cast of characters when a raid occurred in Ellensburg,

Washington. I knew a United Methodist pastor in that city, Rev. Shalom Agtarap as well as Rev. Lyda Pierce who leads the Hispanic ministries for United Methodist churches in Washington State. They witnessed firsthand the fear immigrants were experiencing as a result of the raid by Immigration and Customs Enforcement (ICE) officials as children were coming home from school to find their parents had been detained and they might never see them again. I cannot even begin to fathom what the children in that immigrant community in Ellensburg must have experienced that horrible day. In addition, the weight placed on the faith communities and leaders like Shalom and Lyda in caring for the immigrants left behind was enormous.

So, even in the midst of the tremendous tasks before them, Shalom and Lyda sent me a list of some of the names of the immigrants who had been detained, plus a little bit of information on each as they could find out. At the meeting with the White House and DHS staff just a few days after the raid, rather than following the same meeting protocol which had gotten us nowhere, I began the meeting slowly reading the list of names of the immigrants along with whatever information Shalom and Lyda had sent me. I told them that these were the "criminal aliens" the White House was deporting.

These were good people: fathers, wives, brothers, and sisters, who were doing important work in the community—including day laborers, housewives, and even pastors. When I finished reading the list of names, the entire atmosphere in the room had changed. This was no longer a meeting ABOUT undocumented immigrants. Reading the names and information about the people who had been directly impacted had brought the immigrants into the room with us. Thanks to Shalom and Lyda, the presence of the immigrants through the reading of their names and information was able to counter the lie that raids were solely focused on people who were threats to local communities.

This is the power of creative advocacy. We knew we could not have those families from Ellensburg directly impacted by ICE raids physically with us, but we also knew our own efforts were becoming fruitless. So, we had to creatively find a way for the people directly impacted by injustice to be present and to be heard. It naturally put White House and DHS staff on the defensive and it emboldened the normally jaded DC-based advocates to speak with passion like we hadn't before. The tired line of raids focusing only on "criminal aliens" was bogus and we uncovered the fallacy for all to see. As a faith advocacy community we went on to strenuously object to continued raids. A number of us ultimately engaged in civil disobedience, as I have described previously. As is almost always the case, it is the words, the voices, the stories and the presence of those directly impacted by injustice that changes things. Sometimes you just have to use your imagination and your networks to achieve that presence. But I learned quickly that creative advocacy really does bring about change and effective mobilization.

Now, it is time to take all of what we have discussed, particularly in these last few chapters, and put it together to create a movement for justice so powerful that we see concrete change for people experiencing injustice.

Lessons Recapped:

- Vision and passion will end in success when they are matched with well-devised strategies. Therefore, it is vital that we recognize and use our resources to help us achieve the change we are seeking.

- Strategies are different from plans in that plans are steps to accomplish a goal that does not include influencing a decision-maker. Strategies must not replace the overall vision as the ultimate goal we are seeking to achieve, but strategies are essential for us to make our vision a reality.

- Entrenched power is far more fragile than it appears. As we know the weaknesses those fighting against us we can better highlight our strengths.

- Working for justice will inherently involve conflict so we must engage in confrontations with honesty and boldness and also with genuine invitation for the liberation of those culpable for the injustice.

- People will likely engage in organizing and advocacy when they understand it is consistent with their existing values. This means we must consistently show that advocacy and organizing are biblical and missional and that all of our actions are rooted in incarnational relationships among those directly impacted by injustice.

- We need to honestly assess our resources to mount successful campaigns while employing every ounce of creativity we have, for our resources can be tremendously powerful.

Questions for Discussion:

1. What are the resources that tend to be discounted by faith communities in struggles for justice? Why do these tend not to be valued as as much as other resources such as money or media exposure?

2. Do you agree that entrenched power is actually fragile and can be toppled or undermined? Can you share any current or historical examples to show this?

3. Why, in your opinion, does the faith community struggle with handling conflict in a healthy and constructive way? Have you seen conflict in a church setting handled in a way that was constructive?

4. Do you agree that political advocacy is innovative to many in the church today? What do you believe are reasons for hesitancy in engaging in justice-related ministries?

Idea for Missional Engagement:

Together with your team, begin to map out the resources your team and your allies have in your struggle to attain justice. Also, you may want to map out the resources of those people or forces who oppose you. We can glean from the wisdom of community development practitioners who employ the ABCD (Asset-Based Community Development) method of building communities by starting from the resources of the community.[3] They develop a capacity inventory where they interview the members of the community (in this case, would-be members of your team and other allied individuals, networks, organizations, and businesses), and they keep a list of all of the resources, skills, and relationships that their allies have for use in the struggle to win concrete change.

For instance, I once met with a small group of mostly undocumented immigrants who lived in a county where the sheriff worked closely with ICE (Immigration and Customs Enforcement) officials and kept the immigrants in their county living in perpetual terror. We began to list some of the resources they had at their disposal in this small group of eight people. I emphasize "began" because as you continue to have one-on-one conversations you will likely identify people not only with passion who share your vision, but who also have resources they will gladly donate to attain the vision of concrete change. This small group of immigrants felt tremendously outmatched and overwhelmed but as they began to list their resources the feeling changed.

They went through their resources, skills, and relationships and listed everything they could think of that they would use toward their struggle to end the relationship between the sheriff and ICE. The more they discussed, the more resources, skills, and relationships they realized they had access to. They got creative and listed such easily overlooked resources like:

---

3. See, for example, McKnight and Kretzmann, *Building Communities from the Inside Out*. Although I recommend the whole of McKnight and Kretzmann's book, I would suggest reading chapter 1, in particular.

- transportation (for people to get to rallies, information meetings, etc.);
- artistic skills (for making signs, singing at worship services, chanting at marches, etc.);
- leadership skills and the ability to mobilize small groups of others;
- access to youth in several of the schools who felt passionate about immigrant rights;
- access to ministerial networks where allied pastors and clergy and potential allied faith leaders from other faiths could be contacted;
- access to legal help for immigrants already detained (members of partnered churches);
- access to media expertise to publicize events, write op-eds and letters to the editor, etc. (members of partnered churches);
- sense of humor; and
- spiritual care for those involved in this struggle.

Sometimes we too easily overlook this last one. This was just part of a list that became so long we ran out of flip chart paper! Get creative, think expansively, and be sure, once you have your list, to follow up on prioritizing the resources, skills and relationships you have listed with one-on-one conversations to add those who possess the resources, skills and relationships to your team.

8

A Step toward Unleashing

*Putting It All Together—an Organizing
Model Based on the Book of Esther*

Beth Reilly was a stay-at-home mom with three small kids
when she first became aware through media accounts of the
genocide raging in Darfur, Sudan. She was distressed as she read
about the mothers of small children being forced to grab their kids
in a moment's notice, leaving everything they owned behind, and
running for their lives while their husbands were being murdered.
She was most disturbed when reading the accounts of the impact
on young children. Beth had a three-year-old son and she read
about the death of a three-year-old boy. She read of a five-year-old
girl running for her life, seeking safety from bombs and bullets—
Beth had a five-year-old daughter. She could not imagine living
through this tragedy and she also realized that she had to do something to try and help.

Empathizing with the mothers in Darfur only deepened her
own realization that she was so distant from what she was reading about as she lived in safety and relative luxury in her home in
Ft. Wayne, Indiana. She kept thinking that what was happening
to the people in Darfur was simply "not right; we can and must
do something, we can create change, we can have an impact. The
world does not have to be this way. The US can intervene in this
situation and stop the genocide."[1]

1. Interview with Beth Reilly, March 16, 2016.

Beth immediately began to talk with others about what could be done to stop the genocide and bring relief to the women, men, and children in Darfur. She started sharing her passion and her hopes with others she knew. She started with her husband who made the simple suggestion that she write a letter to her Senator, Richard Lugar (R-IN). Coincidentally, Senator Lugar was a fellow United Methodist and was at the time the Chair of the Foreign Relations Committee, the Senate committee with jurisdiction over the Darfur genocide. She wrote Senator Lugar although she also knew that one letter was not going to persuade him to act. He needed to hear from a significant number of his constituents. So, she talked with the pastor of her church.

Her pastor, who could have easily not wanted to have been bothered or to engage in anything political, responded enthusiastically. They used the worship service to take up offerings to provide relief for those suffering in Darfur, they planned prayer times during the worship service to collectively lift up the needs of those experiencing genocide and for an end to the violence, they used bulletin inserts to educate parishioners as to the full scope of what was happening, and they passed around a petition during worship for people to sign urging their Senators, Representative, and Secretary of State Condoleeza Rice to take appropriate actions to stop the genocide. Her pastor then took the materials that were developed for the actions in her church and shared them with other faith communities to use. An Indiana faith network was developing.

As she continued to do more research to find out what was happening and what could be done to stop the genocide her pastor and her passion led her to more connections. She wrote articles for her United Methodist conference newsletter and discovered other United Methodists who were taking action on the genocide in Darfur as well. She became connected with national advocacy groups to help place speakers in faith communities in Indiana to provide avenues for meaningful action. She learned about the importance of media in shaping messages so she wrote letters to the editor and spoke with journalists to generate coverage of what the burgeoning grassroots network on Darfur in Indiana was doing. She helped organize educational events and planned more actions, which brought on even more media coverage. Every step she took toward her vision of seeing the U.S. intervene in Darfur to bring relief to the victims of the genocide brought her closer to others who shared her passion and vision. She learned so much from others who had spent years working on this and similar issues. She quickly became an expert on what needed to be done to generate enough pressure to bring about change.

Her goals became more specific as this growing network put pressure on the Indiana state legislature to divest from companies that were doing business with the Sudanese government. They also convinced Senator Lugar to pass a bill out of the Foreign Relations committee called the Darfur Peace and Accountability Act of 2006. This legislation was designed to impose sanctions against individuals responsible for genocide, war crimes, and crimes against humanity, and to support measures for the protection of civilians and humanitarian operations as well as peace efforts in Darfur. On October 13, 2006 the bill was signed into law by President Bush.

This amazing story of a stay-at-home mom who was moved to take action to try and help moms in Darfur is being repeated on so many different issues in so many other local contexts by so many other people who, regardless of title or position, are taking action, engaging in redemptive advocacy. These are the people who are changing the world. This is the essence of what the story of Esther is all about. All of what we have covered in the book of Esther has brought us to this point.

What We Have Learned

We have reflected on the fact that Scripture shows us in the story of Esther that the problems of poverty and oppression are not the fault of the poor and oppressed, but rather, are rooted in an unjust distribution of resources and an abuse of power. When we focus all of our solutions on "fixing" the behaviors of the poor and oppressed we will leave injustice in place and untouched. Thus, poverty and oppression will only continue.

We have learned that evil is contemplated and accomplished in the dark and private places isolated from public scrutiny under the shroud of power and affluence. Perpetrating evil against people begins with dehumanizing those who are most vulnerable and marginalized. This kind of evil is rooted deeply in ethnocentrism and racism. Evil—whether it takes the form of genocide or mass incarceration—is subtle, but powerful and devastating when it combines racism and power and is allowed to continue unchecked.

On the other hand, righteousness shines brightly and brings together people of diverse backgrounds and interests who share passion for the same vision: overcoming injustice. Righteousness reminds us that we can and must redemptively utilize all of our resources, no matter how few they might be, for the benefit of others. As we do this we, of course, will benefit ourselves too. More than anything, righteousness is about being in right relationship with the Creator and with all of creation. Evil exists because of those in positions of power and affluence who are detached from those who are suffering from the evil being perpetrated. On the other hand, righteousness conquers evil first through the organizing of people directed by injustice and through the incarnational relationships among those directly impacted by those who have connections with decision-makers.

In the last part of our theological reflection we learned that any engagement in justice must emanate from intimate relationships with those experiencing suffering. In fact, when we try and help those who are suffering outside of incarnational relationships we can actually inhibit the justice they need to relieve their suffering. One thing that can stand in the way of incarnation is our lack of geographical proximity to those directly impacted by injustice. We will know we have achieved incarnation among those directly impacted by injustice when there is mutuality; when their hopes are our hopes, their struggles are our struggles, their dreams are our dreams.

Moving into action we learned we must have a vision of where we are going if we want to achieve concrete change. The key questions we must ask ourselves are: what do we want to change, what do we want to build? What, in one year, two years, three years or more, do we specifically and concretely want to see changed? And our vision—as with all we are doing—must originate in incarnational relationships among those directly impacted by injustice.

In order for our vision to become a reality it must be shared. Social change is inherently a work of a collective group, therefore, we must have a team of people around us who share our passion and our vision. Again, it is absolutely imperative that our team include people who are directly impacted by the injustice we hope to change otherwise we might be adding on to those already experiencing injustice the indignity of not being heard. To form and maintain our team requires that we engage others in one-on-one conversations and that people are invited to work with us. No team was ever formed that ever achieved anything that did not include a personal invitation.

Lastly, we talked about the importance of strategies. A vision built on shared passion and a strong team will go nowhere if there is no strategy for how to get there. To devise effective strategies we must identify what obstacles are present to overcome and what resources we have access to. Effective strategies will include gaining knowledge of the weaknesses of the opposition so that we can best use our strengths. Fighting for justice inherently involves conflict—we want something that someone or something else refuses to share and so we must become more comfortable with dealing with conflict in healthy and constructive ways. But it is never healthy to ignore the fact that conflict exists!

The tactics we utilize as part of the overall strategies are limited only by the limits of our imagination and our creative energies. We will sometimes have to be innovative, but people will join us when they see that what we are doing is for the benefit of those directly impacted by injustice and is consistent with their pre-existing values.

Now, we have come to the place where we can put all of this together into a coherent vision of where we want to go and what we want to change. So, I want to offer two final resources that will help us translate our vision for change into strategic steps toward making change a reality.

Naming the Characters

First, I want to invite you and your team to map out the characters from the book of Esther and then contextualize them to the situation you hope to change. I will share from the example I began this chapter with.

King Ahasuerus

The decision-maker, s/he will be the one whose decision(s) will determine whether the change we envision and are working for will actually take place. It is most advantageous to have as much information about the decision-maker as possible; to know what influences them, what they care about, and what will move them in our direction. For Beth, though she started out just wanting to raise awareness and concern for the people of Darfur, her team in Indiana and the national organizations she worked with quickly focused their attention on achieving concrete change; passing the national legislation that was stuck in the Foreign Relations Committee. She found out that Senator Lugar is a committed United Methodist and a responsive Senator to the people of Indiana so therefore could possibly be persuaded through a large direct appeal to move the bill out of committee and to the floor of the Senate. She focused her efforts toward that end and that is what she and others she worked with accomplished.

Mordecai

Those who are directly impacted by the injustice and who will most directly benefit from the change that is created. As discussed previously, the work for creating change must emanate from the Mordecais and they must be engaged in the planning and carrying out of that change. Those of us who are not Mordecais must be incarnated among those directly impacted for that change to be effective and long-lasting.

In Beth's context, where the Mordecais are halfway around the world and there is at the very least an enormous challenge if not impossibility in forming any kind of direct incarnational relationships with them we must be creative in our work to advocate and organize. For Beth and others she worked with, the use of stories, especially to highlight the suffering that the mothers and children were experiencing, were the primary ways they mobilized people of faith throughout Indiana. These were powerful stories and people could not help but actively respond. The use of stories allowed the people she was mobilizing to have to decide if they were to become active players in the story as well. Stories are engaging and demand a response of some kind.

There are other ways as well. Often, for groups that are experiencing similar kinds of suffering, relationships can be formed and a great many ways to serve can be found as members of the group are resettled into other areas of the world as refugees. The "Lost Boys" of Sudan consisted of roughly 20,000 young people who fled Sudan during the Sudanese civil war and many were resettled in the United States. Some of the Lost Boys in the U.S. became excellent spokespersons for the brutality that the people in Darfur were facing. Incarnational relationships are difficult as we have discussed, but they remain the most effective way to engage our congregations in meaningful and genuine service and advocacy while avoiding the trap of colonialism.

Esther

She represents the person or persons making the "ask" to the decision-maker for the change being sought. Esther has a direct line to the king and typically she or someone in a similar position is the best hope of being most persuasive with the King. It does not appear from what we know of Beth's story that there was one primary Esther-type person, which is not out of the norm. For instance, in the story in chapter 6 in Iowa when the clergy flipped Senator Grassley on his stance on sentencing reform, it was a combination of several primary clergy leaders who recruited other faith leaders to sign the petition, the several Bishops who wrote an op-ed, the clergy who participated in a conference call with the Senator and several in-person meetings with the Senator and his staff that ultimately brought about the dramatic change in his position. The Esther-type person or persons will be found as information about the decision-maker (King Ahasuerus) is gained, which makes the process of finding out information crucial.

Hathach

If the Esther is someone we are not personally close to, or if there is a reason why there is distance (such as Mordecai not being allowed to enter past the city gate because he was dressed in sackcloth and ashes), then we need an intermediary between the Mordecais and the Esthers. Often these are people who work for Esther (such as Hathach and the handmaidens and eunuchs in her court), so the Mordecais might not have much say over who their Hathach will be. Thus, it is wise to know as much about the Hathachs as you can—their motivations, their previous experience with the context we are working in, etc.

In Beth's story, it is unclear as to who exactly some of the Hathachs might have been. But if the Hathachs function as connectors then they become crucial in our work to mobilize the Esthers to the kings, or decision-makers. I have seen all too often that when our teams fail to meet directly with the decision-makers or with the Esthers—those with direct links to the decision-makers—we tend to become discouraged and even discount the Hathachs, who usually function as staff for the people in these important positions. But, as Mordecai showed us in his meeting with Hathach, it is our meetings with the Hathachs where crucial information can be shared and gained. We can find out information about either the decision-maker or the Esther if we do not have a close relationship with them already. Asking questions such as these:

- How do they usually make their decisions?
- Who or what influences them as they form their decisions?
- What motivates them or makes them passionate?
- Who or what would help them make their decision, and how can we be of help in this decision-making process?

You might already know the answers to some of these questions, depending on your context, but Hathachs can confirm your preexisting knowledge or can shed further light. The lesson is, do not discount Hathach.

Haman

The person, persons, or forces preventing you from achieving the change you are working toward. Sometimes, especially among the faith community, we are uncomfortable talking about opponents or people or forces allied against us. But if you hope to create change there will be people or forces to stop that change aligned against you. You cannot achieve or create change if there is nothing trying to prevent that change, otherwise there would be nothing to change! So, in our efforts to create change and stop injustice, there will be people or forces (or both) who benefit from that injustice and who will not give up those benefits easily.

Once again, it is not entirely clear from Beth's story of who or what the Hamans were, but if it is anything like any other struggle for justice, the Hamans were present. More often than not,

Hamans function as forces allied against change. Typical Hamans can include

- apathy among people you are trying to mobilize who simply do not want to be bothered by the needs of others;

- entrenched ethnocentrism or even racism, especially when you look at issues like immigration and there is a great well of racist views spilling into the national debate and media coverage;

- those who benefit from the maintenance of the status quo (and sometimes these forces reside in the upper echelons of the church itself);

- obstinate staff opposed to what we are trying to achieve or change and who work for the decision-maker and who refuse to give the decision-maker correct facts or all of the knowledge surrounding the issue, which is exactly how Haman acted in this story; and

- competing justice issues, which is sadly what happens when there is so much injustice occurring in the world and there is a need to mobilize faith communities to engage in so many ways on so many different issues. There is only so much faith communities can do, so choosing where and in whom you invest your time and energy, relationships, and passion can be an excruciating experience.

These are just some of the Hamans I have run into, but I am sure there are others as Hamans function as obstacles to the concrete change we hope to create. I have seen the obstacles even come from supposed allies as they, for various reasons, become obstacles because they simply do not value advocating for justice or they fear the repercussions of taking on the powerful interests that benefit from an unjust status quo. The critical point to make here is that the Hamans are real and we cannot hope to achieve justice by simply ignoring them. It is imperative that we recognize who or what they are and strategize to address them in some way.

Utilizing Strategy as Steps toward Change

The second resource that I would highly recommend you to take advantage of, and one I have used liberally throughout this book, is the strategy chart found in *Organizing for Social Change*, created by the Midwest Academy Manual for Activists. Though I strongly believe that the greatest teacher we will have in advocating and organizing for change is our own experience of trying and failing and trying again, there is much wisdom to glean from these pages and from the organizers at Midwest Academy.

This tool is something I have seen used by many groups as they have charted their strategies for how to achieve concrete change.[2] Like all resources, you must get a feel for this and then contextualize it for your situation. But here is how I have used it. I will list the specific steps below which will include the changes I have adapted to the chart that I have found useful. For the actual chart as Midwest has it, I encourage you to buy the book itself and read the entire chapter in which it is located.

1. **Goals**

   List the changes you want to make that will make concrete and tangible changes that will improve peoples' lives. Try to think in terms of timelines, which are crucial to have. How long will it take you to achieve concrete change? A hint on timelines is that the closer the change you seek is to your local community the less the amount of time it will take. For instance, achieving citizenship for undocumented immigrants will take much longer because it is a national issue than will trying to pass an ordinance in a city council.

2. **Organizational or Congregational Resources**

   List the resources or assets that your organization or congregation brings to this campaign for concrete change. These can include facilities, money, institutional memory, pastoral care, professional expertise (thinking of specific members of the congregation and what they can contribute), staff, etc.

---

2. Bobo, Kendall, and Max, *Organizing for Social Change*, 33.

We did this at the end of the last chapter so this list should be readily at hand.

3. **Allies and Opponents**

This comes directly from our previous exercise where we contextualized the characters of the Esther story to our situation. Here you ask, who are our allies? Who or what specific groups are touched by the problem we face, who or what specific groups will benefit from the change that we seek, and what potential resources do they have that will add to the campaign we are undertaking? And, as stated above, if we seek to make concrete change we will have opponents and we must recognize this and name them. So, we want to know who or what will not benefit from the concrete change we want to make, how strong are they and what resources do they have that they will use to stop us?

4. **Campaign Focus**

This is the decision-maker who holds the power over whether the concrete change we hope to create will happen or not. This could involve a series of decision-makers, but that will require a complex campaign with a number of mini-campaigns to lead us to achieve the change we hope to create. The more complex our campaign is the more it will lengthen our timeline and will necessitate a greater number of resources and a greater number of allies (as well as possible opponents). Regardless, it is imperative, as we discussed previously in the section on Hathachs, that we know as much information about the decision-maker(s) and those around them as possible so that we can best craft a successful campaign.

5. **Tactics**

The tactics are the steps we take toward achieving the concrete change we hope to create. Tactics are focused solely on changing the mind of the decision-maker to take the action we want them to take. Tactics can and should be creative, organic, contextual, specific, and directed toward the decision-maker to convince them to take the action we need. Throughout this book I have tried to share stories that show a variety of tactics that churches have used to achieve concrete change. The possible tactics can include (but do not necessarily need to be limited to)

- media outreach such as letters to the editor, op-ed's, or press conferences;
- call-ins to decision-makers,
- in-person meetings with decision-makers with various constituencies present,
- public hearings with those directly impacted serving as witnesses so that awareness is raised and knowledge about the injustice is amassed,
- prayer vigils,
- town hall sessions with the decision-makers,
- letter-a-day campaigns from various allied organizations, etc.

It is important that the tactic not become more important than the strategy. It is also important that these actions, when possible, be coordinated with other faith communities and engaged organizations so that the impact can be most effective. Lastly, what makes tactics most effective is timing. We will know when to use specific tactics the more information we have about what influences the decision-maker.

The two resources I have shared—naming the characters from Esther and utilizing the strategy chart—can increase the chances for success for your campaign to achieve concrete change for people experiencing injustice, but I strongly urge you not to think that following steps will alone ensure success. I believe with every fiber of my being that utilizing the strategy chart or contextualizing the characters from Esther to your situation will only be effective if you have spent the necessary time sharpening and developing our vision through one-on-one conversations, inviting others to share their passion with ours, and most of all, taking the necessary time to build incarnational relationships with those directly impacted by injustice. There is nothing that can replace the importance of these basic formational steps and no chart or training can substitute for the basis of our engagement in justice and our hope for God's Kingdom to be realized on earth. The greatest truth we can learn and live out is that the basis of any concrete change we achieve is relationships.

The Last Word

One thing I have tried hard to do throughout this project is to lift up the work of normal, everyday folks. Folks who do not get a lot of attention or receive a lot of awards, who don't get asked to speak all over the country or asked by media outlets to wax eloquently about their thoughts on needed changes in the world. I have focused on local folks who create change every day, who transform the world every day through their love for people who are directly impacted by systems of injustice. These people amaze me. These are the people with whom I have worked closely and from whom I have learned so much. These are my heroes and these are the folks I have dedicated this book to.

In the decade that I've worked on a national level primarily with United Methodists, there is one belief that has become deeply entrenched in me: I believe that local churches are the locus of God's transformational work in the world. Local churches are where people experience missional engagement, recognition of their own privilege and prejudice, and the grace of repentance from racism, classism, sexism, agism, and other debilitating forms of relational death. It is in the local church where one finds the wonderful invitation to follow Jesus into liberating, incarnational relationships among people directly impacted by injustice. God wants to change the world and I believe that God will do it from the ground up.

One of the greatest mistakes in our denominations today is to believe that change emanates from the top down. This is seen in the idea that change will be a project initiated by the bishops, cared for by national agencies and committees, and then with the assumption that local churches will follow those mandates almost mindlessly. This kind of institutional elitism permeates not only the upper echelons of denominational churches; sadly, it permeates and even paralyzes local churches as well. I have seen personally and I believe Scripture bears witness to the fact that the most powerful and effective change begins locally and flows upward rather than the other way around. Our entire faith as Christians is grounded in the birth of an obscure baby in the Middle East, whose parents were forced to flee to Africa to escape an infanticide.

I began my work on the national level of the United Methodist Church having come to that position from serving in local churches since I was a student at McMurry University. I believed in the power of the local church and I arrived in Washington, DC, still believing that local churches were the primary places that could and would most clearly minister the good news of God's Kingdom being manifest on earth.

In the early fall of 2007 I was in Iowa where more than thirty-five candidates for president were beginning their run in the Iowa Caucuses, which were set to happen in January 2008. As I visited with United Methodists and other people of faith there, they let me know that the rhetoric around the issue of immigration by presidential candidates was horrible to listen to. And it wasn't just the Republicans either, both sides constantly referred to immigrants as "illegals" and there was a sense that all of the candidates just assumed that all Iowans agreed with the constant barrage being levelled against immigrants.

Well, they didn't all agree. I remember talking with an amazing woman, Doris Knight, a grandmother, a member of an amazing church called Trinity/Las Americas United Methodist Church, and the site director for the Iowa Justice for Our Neighbors (JFON), a United Methodist-run ministry offering free legal help to low-income immigrants. Doris was upset about the rancor of the campaigns and wanted to do something about it. We talked about how faith people should be more coordinated in making their voices heard and so we decided on doing a petition signed by people of faith that recognized the contributions immigrants made to Iowa and the entire country. I asked her to gather as many people as she could from as many different faith communities for a call and I returned to DC.

Doris is a sweet, caring woman of God, but she is as passionate as they come; fierce even. She gathered people from every faith community she could find who had any interest in loving and welcoming immigrants, including Connie Ryan, who heads the Interfaith Alliance of Iowa and who provided the statewide leadership as well as technical assistance we needed to make this truly a statewide and interfaith effort. I was shocked when the time for the call came that so many people were on and passionately ready to do something. Doris had done the hard work of contacting people one-on-one and inviting them to join in this important effort. It took us a few weeks to figure out language for the petition and other logistics, but by the beginning of November the petition was up and ready to go.

We were hoping, if we got enough signatures, to have a press event by early December, so we had the month of November to gather signatures—less than a full month, really, given the Thanksgiving holiday. Jen Smyers, a colleague at the national office of Church World Service, and I spent a week in Iowa visiting folks and speaking to faith groups, but there is no question that the more than 3,000 signatures we ended up with were the result of the hard work and tenacity of the local faith communities who believed immigrants are our sisters and brothers and should not be demonized by people running for the highest office in the country.

After the press event, which was covered by national media outlets, the teams split up to hand-deliver copies of the petitions to every campaign office. Some workers were in the offices and some were not. But the most memorable meeting was the delivery to then-Senator Obama's campaign office. They actually met with Senator Obama for a few minutes and then with his campaign staff. The staff agreed to change the wording in his speeches and his literature in referring to immigrants from "illegal" to "undocumented." As far as I know, he has never used "illegal" since that time. For a brief time at least, the story when it came to immigration was not about the candidates promising tougher borders and increased deportations. For a short time, the story was about the people of faith in Iowa who valued the presence and contributions of immigrants and were tired of the constant dehumanizing rhetoric.

This is the story that we are called to join: that we are called to bring about concrete change for and with people who are experiencing injustice. We have the resources to make change. We only need the vision and passion, rooted in our relationships among those directly impacted by injustice to see those visions to the end. May the God of justice and love grant you the power of the Holy Spirit to work for justice until you have no steps to walk, no air to breathe. And then may we walk into God's Kingdom to celebrate the fullness of the reality of what we hoped for and envisioned while on earth.

Bibliography

Alexander, Michelle. *The New Jim Crow: Mass Incarceration in the Age of Colorblindness.* New York: New Press, 2010.

Alinsky, Saul D. *Rules for Radicals.* New York: Vintage, 1971.

Birch, Bruce C., and Larry L. Rasmussen. *The Predicament of the Prosperous.* Philadelphia: Westminster, 1978.

Bobo, Kim, Jackie Kendall, and Steve Max. *Organizing for Social Change: Midwest Academy Manual for Activists.* 4th ed. Santa Ana, CA: Forum Press, 2010.

Davis, David Brion. *Inhuman Bondage: The Rise and Fall of Slavery in the New World.* New York: Oxford University Press, 2006.

Dayton, Donald. *Discovering an Evangelical Heritage.* Peabody, MA: Hendrickson, 1976.

Dietterich, Inagrace T. "Missional Community: Cultivating Communities of the Holy Spirit." In *Missional Church: A Vision for the Sending of the Church in North America,* edited by Darrell L. Guder, 142–82. Grand Rapids: Eerdmans, 1998.

Dillard, Raymond, and Tremper Longman. *An Introduction to the Old Testament.* Grand Rapids: Zondervan, 1994.

Dittmer, John. *Local People: The Struggle for Civil Rights in Mississippi.* Urbana: University of Illinois Press, 1995.

Emerson, Michael O., and Christian Smith. *Divided by Faith: Evangelical Religion and the Problem of Race in America.* New York: Oxford University Press, 2000.

Fox, Michael V. *Character and Ideology in the Book of Esther.* Grand Rapids: Eerdmans, 2001.

Gaebelein, Frank E., ed. *The Expositor's Bible Commentary.* Vol. 4: *1 & 2 Kings, 1 & 2 Chronicles, Ezra, Nehemiah. Esther, Job.* Grand Rapids: Zondervan, 1988.

Gordon, Wayne L. *Real Hope in Chicago.* Grand Rapids: Zondervan, 1995.

Gutiérrez, Gustavo. *A Theology of Liberation.* Maryknoll, NY: Orbis, 1973.

Katz, Michael B. *The Undeserving Poor: From the War on Poverty to the War on Welfare.* New York: Pantheon, 1989.

Kotz, Nick. *Judgment Days: Lyndon Baines Johnson, Martin Luther King Jr., and the Laws That Changed America.* New York: Houghton Mifflin, 2005.

Kruse, Kevin M. *White Flight: Atlanta and the Making of Modern Conservatism.* Princeton: Princeton University Press, 2005.

Leffel, Gregory P. *Faith Seeking Action: Mission, Social Movements, and the Church in Motion.* Lanham, MD: Scarecrow, 2007.

Mauer, Marc, and Meda Chesney-Lind, eds. *Invisible Punishment: The Collateral Consequences of Mass Imprisonment.* NewYork: Norton, 2002.

McAdam, Doug. *Freedom Summer.* New York: Oxford University Press, 1988.

McKnight, John L., and John P. Kretzmann. *Building Communities from the Inside Out: A Path toward Finding and Mobilizing a Community's Assets.* Skokie, IL: ACTA, 1993.

Mefford, William Richard, "To Set Free the Affluent: Liberating the North American Church in Captivity through Solidarity with Refugees." Doctor of Missiology diss., Asbury Theological Seminary, 2008.

Memmi, Albert. *The Colonizer and the Colonized.* Boston: Beacon, 1965.

Moberg, David O. *The Great Reversal: Evangelism versus Social Concern.* Philadelphia: Lippincott, 1972.

Moe-Lobeda, Cynthia D. *Healing a Broken World: Globalization and God.* Minneapolis: Fortress, 2002.

Payne, Charles M. *I've Got the Light of Freedom: The Organizing Tradition and the Mississippi Freedom Struggle.* Berkeley: University of California Press, 1995.

Rieger, Joerg. *Globalization and Theology.* Nashville: Abingdon, 2010.

Rogers, Everett M. *Diffusion of Innovations.* New York: Simon & Schuster, 1995.

Sen, Rinku. *Stir It Up: Lessons in Community Organizing and Advocacy.* San Francisco: Jossey-Bass, 2003.

Shaw, Randy. *The Activist's Handbook: A Primer.* Berkeley: University of California Press, 2001.

Silver, James W. *Mississippi: The Closed Society.* New York: Harcourt, Brace & World, 1963.

Slessarev-Jamir, Helene. *Prophetic Activism: Progressive Religious Justice Movements in Contemporary America.* New York: New York Universty Press, 2011.

Solomon, Robert C., and Mark C. Murphy. *What Is Justice?* New York: Oxford University Press, 1990.

United Nations Center for Human Settlements. *Cities in a Globalizing World: Global Report on Human Settlements 2001.* Sterling, VA: Earthscan, 2001.

Volf, Miroslav. *Exclusion & Embrace: A Theological Exploration of Identity, Otherness, and Reconciliation.* Nashville: Abingdon, 1996.

Wogaman, J. Philip. *Christian Perspectives on Politics.* 2nd ed. Louisville: Westminster John Knox, 2000.

Woodward, C. Vann. *The Strange Career of Jim Crow.* New York: Oxford University Press, 1974 ca. 1955.

Yoder, John Howard. *The Politics of Jesus.* 2nd ed. Grand Rapids: Zondervan, 1994.